How to Use History Pockets

In *History Pockets—Ancient Civilizations,* young learners get their first glimpses at the fascinating accomplishments of six ancient cultures. The engaging activities are stored in labeled pockets and bound into a decorative cover. Students will be proud to see their accumulated projects presented all together. At the end of the book, evaluation sheets have been added for teacher use.

Make a Pocket

1. Use a 12″ x 18″ (30.5 x 45.5 cm) piece of construction paper for each pocket. Fold up 6″ (15 cm) to make a 12″ (30.5 cm) square.
2. Staple the right side of each pocket closed.
3. Punch two or three holes in the left side of each pocket.

Assemble the Pocket Book

1. Reproduce the cover illustration on page 3 for each student.
2. Direct students to color and cut out the illustration and glue it onto a 12″ (30.5 cm) square of construction paper to make the cover.
3. Punch two or three holes in the left side of the cover.
4. Fasten the cover and the pockets together. You might use string, ribbon, twine, raffia, or binder rings.

Every Pocket Has...

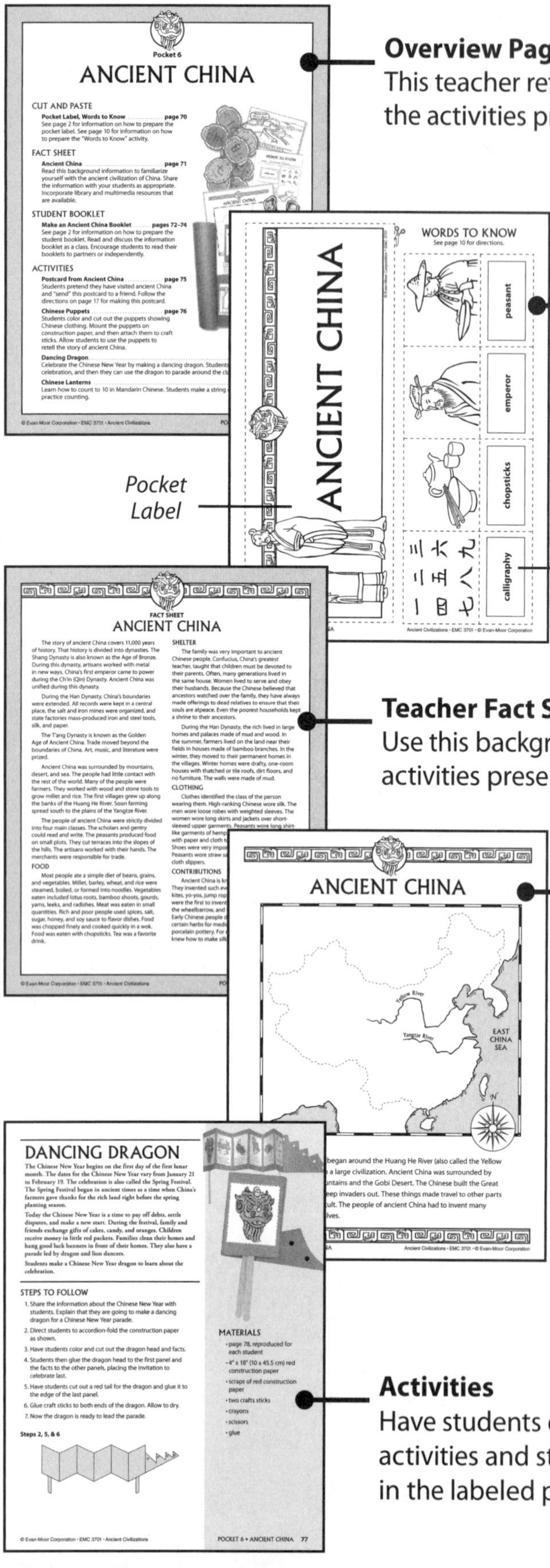

Overview Page
This teacher reference page describes the activities presented in each pocket.

Pocket Label and Words to Know
Reproduce the page for students. Direct students to color and cut out the pocket label and glue it onto the pocket. Have students use the Words to Know to make a picture dictionary, following the directions on page 10.

Teacher Fact Sheet
Use this background information as a reference for the activities presented in the pocket.

Student Booklet
Reproduce the pages to make an information booklet for each student. Staple the booklet to a 9″ x 12″ (23 x 30.5 cm) piece of construction paper for durability.

Activities
Have students do the activities and store them in the labeled pocket.

Note: Reproduce this cover for students to color, cut out, and glue to the cover of their Ancient Civilizations book.

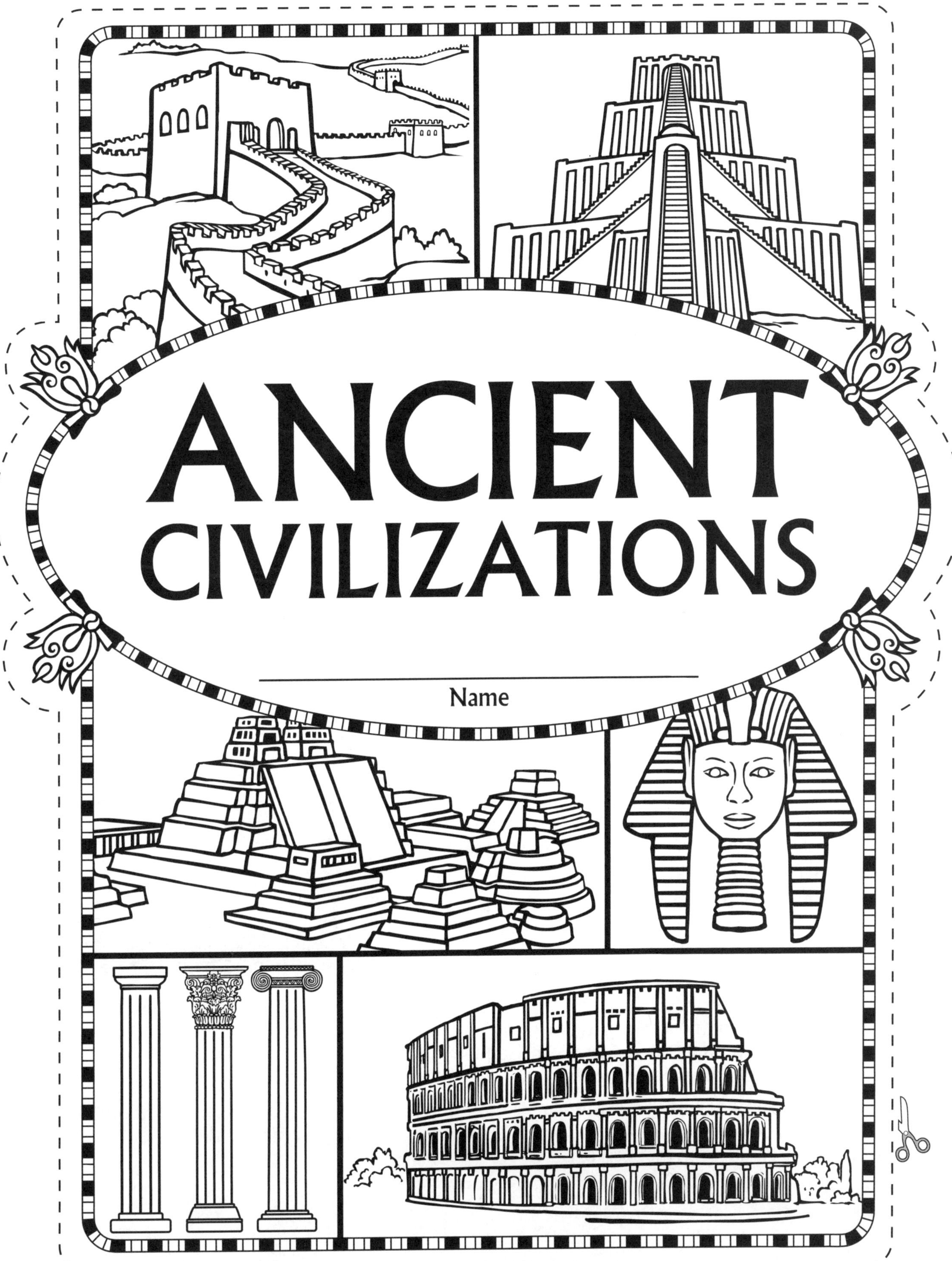

Pocket 1

WHAT IS HISTORY?

CUT AND PASTE

Pocket Label, Words to Know................ **page 5**
See page 2 for information on how to prepare the pocket label. See page 10 for information on how to prepare the "Words to Know" activity.

FACT SHEET

What Is History?............................. **page 6**
Read and share this background information about the study of history with your students as appropriate.

STUDENT BOOKLET

Make a "What Is History?" Booklet....... **pages 7–9**
See page 2 for information on how to prepare the student booklet. Read and discuss the information booklet as a class. Encourage students to read their booklets to partners or independently.

ACTIVITIES

Words to Know......................... **pages 10–12**
In this pocket students begin a "Words to Know" picture dictionary using the words presented on the pocket label page. A picture dictionary page is included in each pocket.

Map of Ancient Civilizations................ **page 13**
Reproduce the map for each student to place in the pocket. As you begin each new civilization, locate its area on the map.

When Did It Happen? .... **pages 14–16**
Introduce chronological thinking with a lesson on time—past, present, and future. Students use word cards to learn how to identify the sequence in which events occurred in history. Then students put together a simplified time line of the ancient civilizations.

Postcards from Ancient Civilizations.. **page 17**
As each new civilization is studied, have students write a postcard to a friend telling about a famous structure from that part of history.

WHAT IS HISTORY?

WORDS TO KNOW

See page 10 for directions.

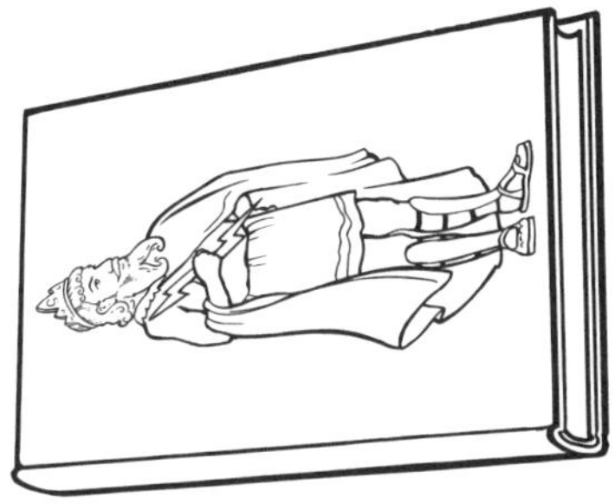

history

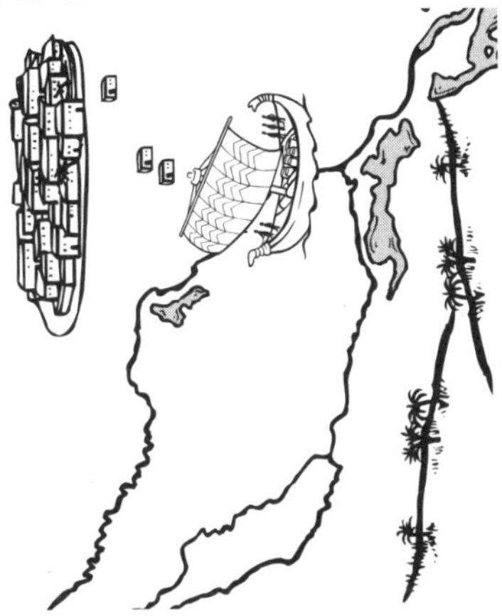

civilization

basic needs

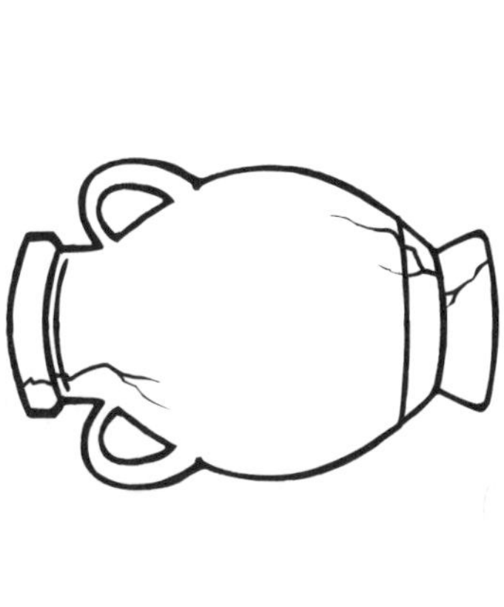

ancient

FACT SHEET

WHAT IS HISTORY?

The study of the past is called history. To study ancient history is to go back thousands of years. To measure this time, historians use the terms B.C. and A.D. The term B.C. stands for *before Christ*. A.D. stands for the Latin words *anno Domini*, which means "in the year of the Lord." Some contemporary scholars use the abbreviations B.C.E. and C.E. The abbreviation B.C.E. stands for *before the common era*, and C.E. stands for *common era*.

Thousands of years ago, people were hunters and gatherers. They followed the food supply from place to place. When people began to learn how to grow their own food, they settled in small groups throughout the world. They learned how to cultivate plants and raise animals for food. It was when these early peoples grew a surplus of food that complex civilizations began to develop.

The rise of more complex ancient civilizations such as Mesopotamia, Egypt, Greece, Rome, China, and the Aztec world had these things in common:

1. Most people built ancient civilizations near rivers or oceans. These water sources provided food and transportation, and made trade with other societies more accessible.
2. The basic needs of food, shelter, and clothing were essential for each society to flourish. They had to have a stable food supply for their people. They all developed some kind of irrigation system for their crops to grow. Houses and clothing were made from available resources.
3. There was a specialization of labor. Most people in all the civilizations were farmers. Other skilled jobs developed as the societies became more sophisticated. People worked together to build public buildings, especially temples for worship of their gods. Craftspeople developed special skills, and new inventions arose to make everyday life easier.
4. All of the civilizations had their own system of government. They had leaders who made rules so that life in the civilization would run smoothly.
5. Each civilization had social levels. Usually there were three social levels in a society. At the top were the most powerful—rulers, government officials, and priests. The second level was usually made up of merchants, laborers, farmers, and craftspeople. At the bottom of the social scale were enslaved people, who often were captured in battle.
6. All of these civilizations had a highly developed culture. This included art, architecture, music, and other forms of entertainment.
7. They all developed their own system of writing. Usually only a few educated or trained members of the society were able to write, so these scribes became important and powerful.
8. All of the civilizations had their own kind of religion. Polytheism, the belief in many gods, was common throughout the ancient world.

These common characteristics are reflected in all six ancient civilizations. However, each of these civilizations developed in different parts of the world. Ancient Mesopotamia developed in the Middle East, while ancient Egypt grew powerful in northern Africa. Ancient Greece and ancient Rome developed in southern Europe and because of the close proximity fought for control of this part of the world. The highly developed society of ancient China had little contact with the outside world, but was still able to flourish. The ancient Aztecs developed their complex society in Central America.

It is important to study these ancient civilizations so we can see the connection between the past and present. We can learn how people from different time periods and different parts of the world lived.

WHAT IS HISTORY?

5,000 Years Ago

ANCIENT MESOPOTAMIA

The ziggurat was built.

4,000 Years Ago

ANCIENT EGYPT

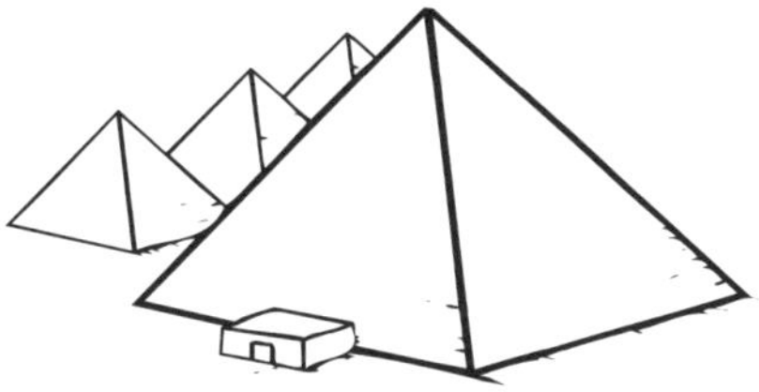

The pyramids were built.

3,000 Years Ago

ANCIENT GREECE

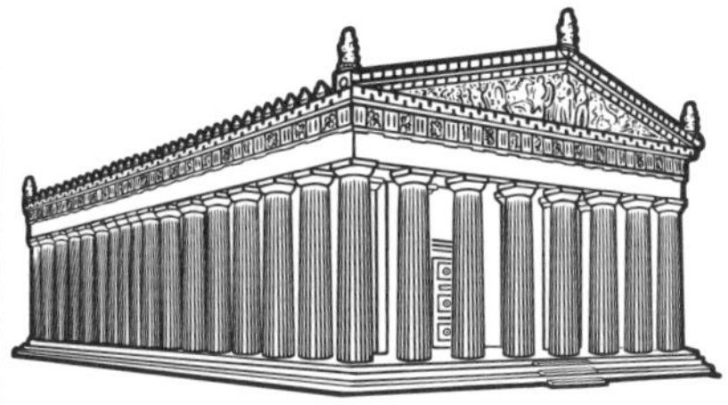

The Parthenon was built.

2,000 Years Ago

ANCIENT ROME

The Colosseum was built.

1,000 Years Ago

ANCIENT CHINA

The Great Wall of China was built.

500 Years Ago

ANCIENT AZTEC WORLD

The Great Temple was built.

History is the study of the past. We study history to learn about the people who lived long ago. We learn about the things that happened to them. We learn about inventions they made. We study history to see that people who lived long ago were like us. We also learn that they were different from us in other ways.

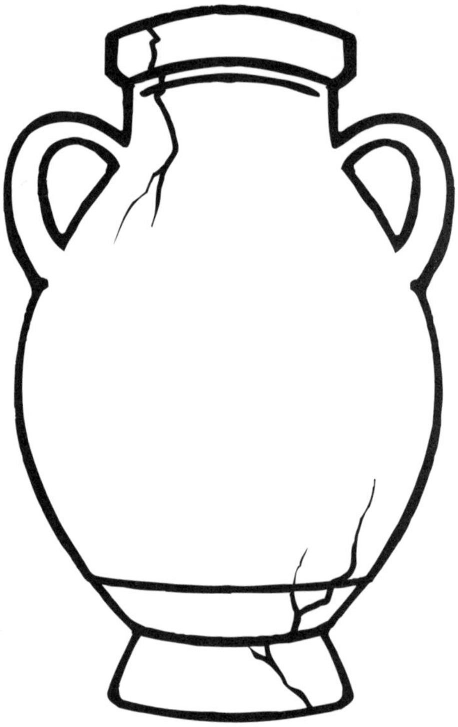

Ancient history is the study of long, long ago. The word **ancient** means "very, very old." Thousands of years ago, people developed new civilizations. A **civilization** is a large group of people living and working together in a well-organized way. Ancient civilizations were built in many places such as Mesopotamia, Egypt, Greece, Italy, China, and Mexico.

All of these civilizations had to have the same things. People lived near rivers or oceans. The people had basic needs. The **basic needs** were food, shelter, and clothing. The people had to grow their own food. They built houses using materials that were around them. They wore clothes made from the plants and animals that were in the area.

Every civilization had jobs for their people. They had to have laws. They all had leaders. They had beautiful art and music. Every one of them had their own kind of religion. The people developed their own kind of writing. They had people who invented new things.

Ancient civilizations grew and changed. Thousands of years passed. They left behind clues of their past. Scientists called archeologists dig up everyday objects and treasures. They figure out some of their writing. We learn that people who lived long, long ago were like us in many ways.

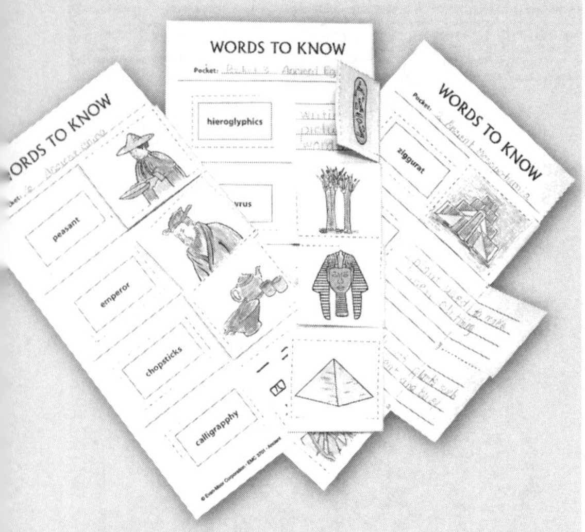

MATERIALS

- page 11, reproduced for each student
- scissors
- glue
- crayons
- stapler

WORDS TO KNOW

As your students learn about the ancient civilizations, have them complete this picture dictionary. Four words are added in each pocket. Reproduce page 11 for each student when a new pocket is started.

STEPS TO FOLLOW

As each pocket is studied, guide students through these steps to complete a Words to Know dictionary page.

1. Color and cut out the pictures and words found on the pocket label page.
2. Glue the four words into the word boxes on page 11.
3. Guide students in writing a definition of each word.

   The Words to Know for each pocket are found in the student booklet.

   After students have read the student booklet, assist them in scanning to find any of the Words to Know. Reread the section containing the word. Help students form a simple definition. (See page 12 for answer key.) Write the definition on the chalkboard for students to copy. More capable students may be able to write the definitions independently after a few pockets.
4. Instruct students to cut on the dotted lines and fold the flaps. Glue the pictures onto the outer flaps.

Step 1

Step 2

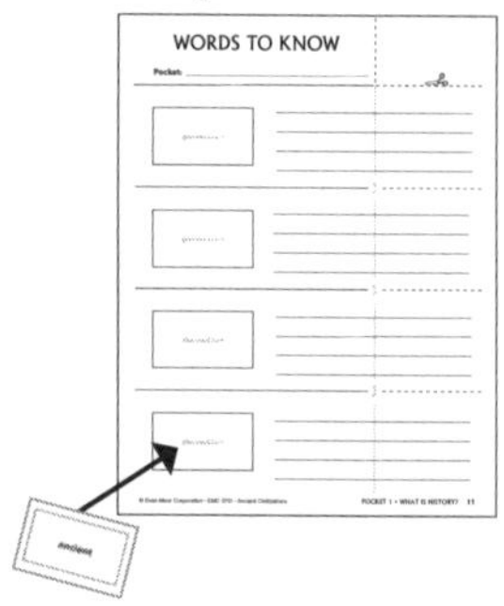

Step 4

WORDS TO KNOW

Pocket: ____________________

glue word here

fold

glue word here

fold

glue word here

fold

glue word here

WORDS TO KNOW

TEACHER ANSWER KEY

Pocket 1—What Is History?

1. **ancient**	very, very old
2. **basic needs**	food, shelter, and clothing
3. **civilization**	the way in which people live together in a large area; all have a stable food supply, work for its people, government, culture (art, architecture, religion, and music), and a system of writing
4. **history**	study of the past

Pocket 2—Ancient Mesopotamia

1. **ziggurat**	a temple tower with a shrine on top
2. **flax**	from the stems of this plant used to make clothing; linen
3. **grains**	seeds of cereal plants such as wheat and barley
4. **city-state**	an area made up of a city, surrounding villages, and farmland

Pocket 3—Ancient Egypt

1. **pyramid**	a stone structure built as a tomb
2. **pharaoh**	a ruler or king of ancient Egypt
3. **papyrus**	a long, thin reed used to make paper
4. **hieroglyphics**	a writing system in which pictures stand for words or sounds

Pocket 4—Ancient Greece

1. **agora**	a marketplace
2. **chiton**	wool or linen tunics
3. **columns**	tall pillars that support or decorate a building
4. **myth**	an ancient story that tries to explain how the world became the way it is

Pocket 5—Ancient Rome

1. **empire**	a nation and its city-states and nations it has conquered, under one ruler
2. **Roman numerals**	a number system in which letters stand for numbers
3. **forum**	a marketplace, government buildings, and temples located in the center of a city
4. **toga**	a long white robe

Pocket 6—Ancient China

1. **calligraphy**	an ancient form of writing using brush and ink
2. **chopsticks**	a pair of thin sticks used as eating tools
3. **emperor**	a ruler of ancient China
4. **peasant**	a farmer

Pocket 7—Ancient Aztec World

1. **chinampas**	floating gardens
2. **temple**	a building used for religious worship
3. **tortillas**	round, flat bread made from cornmeal
4. **knight**	the highest ranking warrior

Note: Reproduce this page for students to use with "Map of Ancient Civilizations," as described on page 4.

Map of Ancient Civilizations

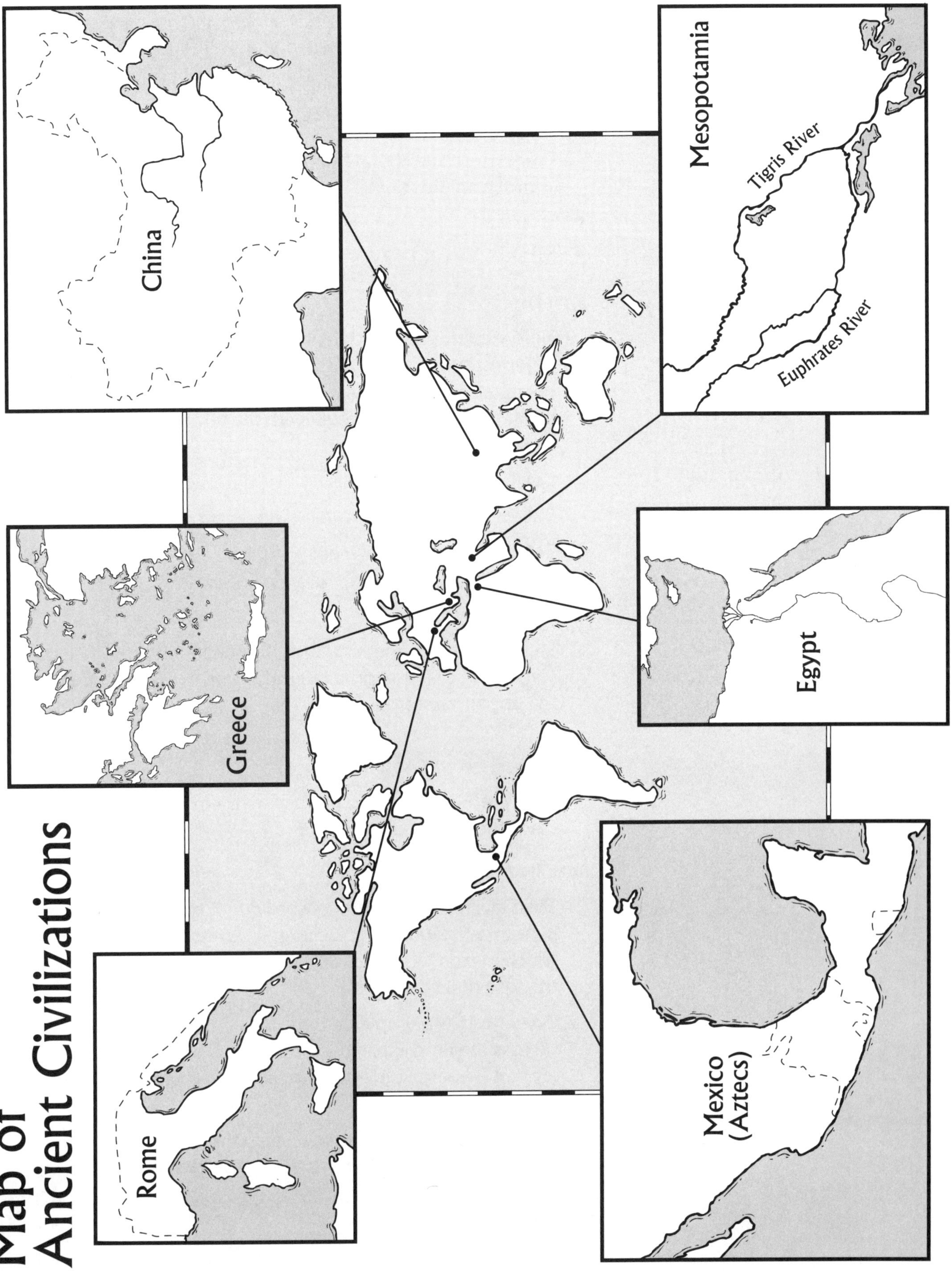

MATERIALS

- pages 15 and 16, reproduced for each student
- pencil
- crayons
- scissors
- glue or transparent tape
- envelopes

WHEN DID IT HAPPEN?

With a sense of historical time, students are able to see relationships between events. Placing events in chronological order gives students a sense of the past, present, and future. Then students put together a simple time line of important monuments that were built during the ancient civilizations.

STEPS TO FOLLOW

Part One

1. Help students begin to think chronologically. Make a class demonstration set of cards from page 15. It would be helpful to enlarge the cards or make an overhead transparency. As a class, order the word cards. Begin with the terms most familiar to your students.

Set 1:	yesterday	today	tomorrow
Set 2:	last year	this year	next year
Set 3:	past	present	future

2. Distribute copies of page 15 for students to use for the writing activity.

   Students write something that happened to them yesterday, something that is happening today, and something that is going to happen tomorrow. Follow that same procedure for sets 2 and 3.

3. Share their writings in class.
4. After cutting the words apart, store them in envelopes and place them in the first pocket.

Part Two

1. Then talk further about the word *past*. Explain to students that in history the word *past* includes *long ago* and *long, long ago,* which means "hundreds and thousands of years ago." We refer to those times as *ancient*.
2. On page 16 is a simplified time line of the ancient civilizations. Discuss the time line with students, and then have them color and cut it apart. Students then glue or tape the time line together.
3. Have students place the time line in the first pocket. Use as reference for the students as you study each civilization.

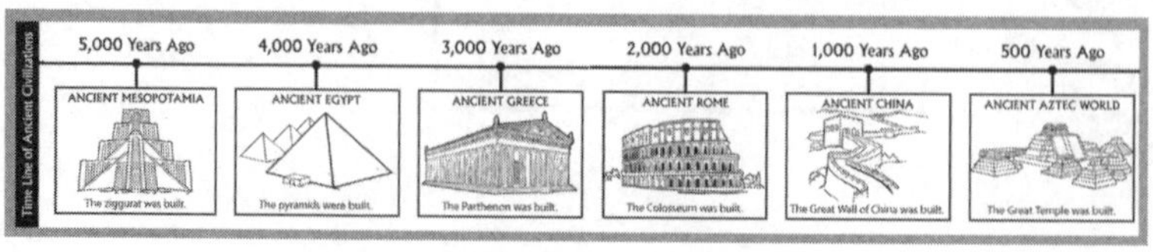

WHEN DID IT HAPPEN?

YESTERDAY	TODAY	TOMORROW
LAST YEAR	THIS YEAR	NEXT YEAR
PAST	PRESENT	FUTURE

TIME LINE OF ANCIENT CIVILIZATIONS

Time Line of Ancient Civilizations

5,000 Years Ago

ANCIENT MESOPOTAMIA

The ziggurat was built.

4,000 Years Ago

ANCIENT EGYPT

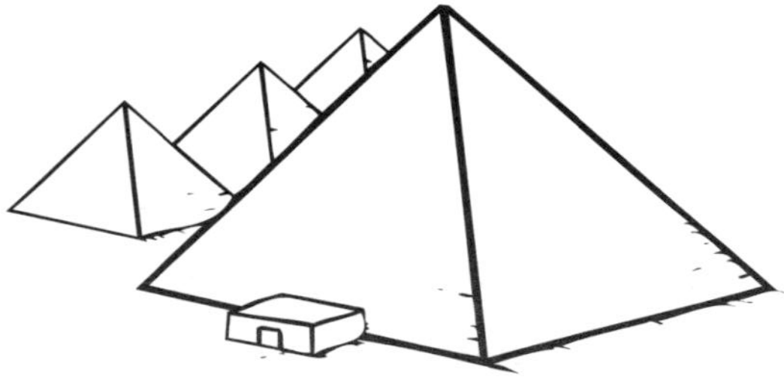

The pyramids were built.

3,000 Years Ago

ANCIENT GREECE

The Parthenon was built.

glue here

2,000 Years Ago

ANCIENT ROME

The Colosseum was built.

1,000 Years Ago

ANCIENT CHINA

The Great Wall of China was built.

500 Years Ago

ANCIENT AZTEC WORLD

The Great Temple was built.

POSTCARDS FROM ANCIENT CIVILIZATIONS

Students will "send" a postcard to a friend each time they visit a new civilization.

MATERIALS

- postcard patterns for each civilization, reproduced for each student
- pencil
- crayons
- scissors
- stapler

STEPS TO FOLLOW

1. As you study each new civilization, reproduce the postcard pattern that corresponds to that particular civilization. (See pages 24, 38, 50, 64, 75, and 88.) Each postcard shows a major historical monument from that civilization.
2. Have students color the picture and read the caption on the postcard.
3. On the other side of the postcard, have students write a message to a friend telling them about the picture or something interesting about the civilization.
4. Instruct students to address the postcard and design a stamp.
5. Direct students to cut out the postcard on the dotted lines.
6. Have students fold the postcard and then staple on both sides to make a two-sided postcard.
7. Now they are ready to "send" the postcard to a friend.

Pocket 2

ANCIENT MESOPOTAMIA

CUT AND PASTE

Pocket Label, Words to Know............... **page 19**
See page 2 for information on how to prepare the pocket label. See page 10 for information on how to prepare the "Words to Know" activity.

FACT SHEET

Ancient Mesopotamia .... **page 20**
Read this background information to familiarize yourself with the ancient civilization of Mesopotamia. Share the information with your students as appropriate. Incorporate library and multimedia resources that are available.

STUDENT BOOKLET

Make an Ancient Mesopotamia Booklet .... **pages 21–23**
See page 2 for information on how to prepare the student booklet. Read and discuss the information booklet as a class. Encourage students to read their booklets to partners or independently.

ACTIVITIES

Postcard from Ancient Mesopotamia .... **page 24**
Students pretend they have visited ancient Mesopotamia and "send" this postcard to a friend. Follow the directions on page 17 for making this postcard.

Mesopotamian Puppets .... **page 25**
Students color and cut out the puppets showing Mesopotamian clothing. Mount the puppets on construction paper, and then attach them to craft sticks. Allow students to use the puppets to retell the story of Mesopotamia.

Sailing on the River .... **pages 26–28**
Students learn about the importance of the Tigris and the Euphrates Rivers to Mesopotamian travel and trade. Students make a sailboat to travel down the Tigris River.

Ziggurat Pop-up Book .... **pages 29–31**
Students make a pop-up book of a ziggurat and read interesting facts about this Mesopotamian temple.

ANCIENT

MESOPOTAMIA

WORDS TO KNOW

See page 10 for directions.

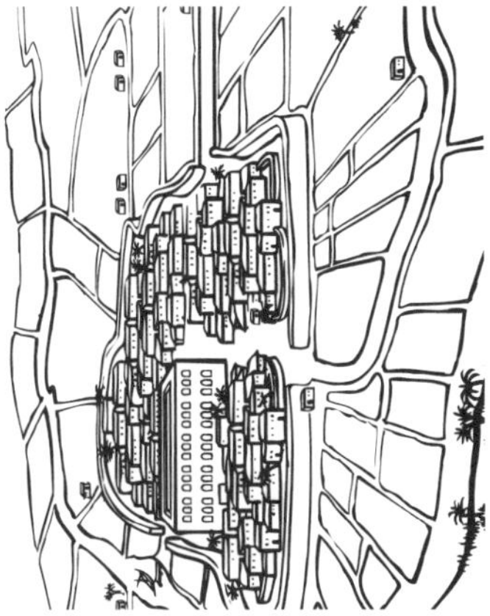

city-state

grains

flax

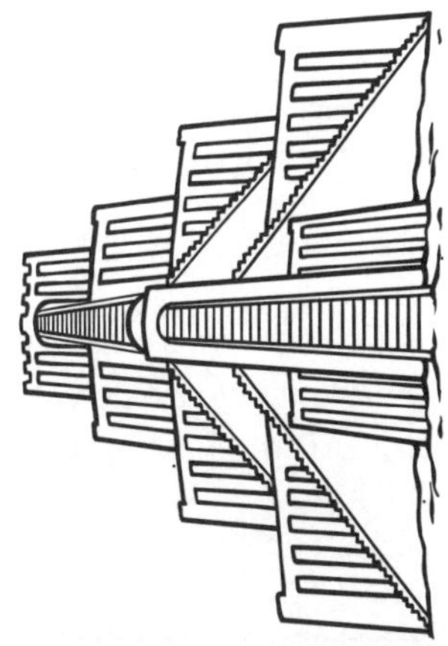

ziggurat

FACT SHEET

ANCIENT MESOPOTAMIA

Historians believe that the Mesopotamian settlement of Sumer represents the world's first civilization. For this reason, Mesopotamia is often referred to as the "cradle of civilization." Their civilization spanned from about 3500 B.C. to 1900 B.C. The name *Mesopotamia* comes from the Greek language and means "the land between two rivers." Nomadic peoples settled in the area where the Tigris the Euphrates Rivers met. This area is in the present-day Iraq and parts of Syria and Turkey.

The Mesopotamian plain had very hot summers, little rain, and dry land. However, the spring rains brought flooding to the rivers. The flooding spread rich soil that helped to grow wheat and barley. The Mesopotamians created irrigation systems to bring the water from the rivers to the plains. Because they were able to grow crops, the Mesopotamians were then able to build their city-states.

The Mesopotamians became traders, as their farmers were able to produce more food than they needed. They used riverboats called turnips to transport goods. They developed a system of recordkeeping to manage their trade, developed the wheel and the sailboat to help move heavy items, and set up formal contracts on clay tablets using their wedge-writing called cuneiform. In 1900 B.C., Amorites from the Syrian Desert conquered Sumer. Hammurabi became the powerful king of Mesopotamia and introduced an important code of law.

FOOD

Mesopotamian farmers became the granary of the ancient world. Farmers grew wheat and barley and other food crops. The people of Mesopotamia enjoyed barley cakes, flatbread, and barley beer. They fished and hunted in the marshes along the rivers.

SHELTER

The earliest Mesopotamian homes were huts built from bundles of reeds. Later homes were built from sun-baked mud bricks. Homes were built radiating from the all-important city center—the temple. Upper-class homes were two-storied. Lower-class homes were one-story. A brick wall surrounded the homes in the city-state. Farmland belonging to the city-state was outside the wall.

The temple in the center of each city-state housed the city-state's patron god or goddess. Originally, the temples were built on a platform. As time passed, these platform temples became the temple-towers called ziggurats. *Ziggurat* means "mountain of god or hill of heaven." Ziggurats were pyramidal structures built of sun-baked bricks. The facings of the structure were made of colorful glazed bricks.

CLOTHING

Mesopotamians made their clothing from the natural resources available to them. Cloth was made from wool or flax. Men were bare-chested and wore skirtlike garments that tied at the waist. Women usually wore gowns that covered them from their shoulders to their ankles. The right arm and shoulder were left uncovered. Women braided their hair and wrapped it around their heads. They wore headdresses in their hair for important occasions. Both wealthy men and women wore gold and silver jewelry set with precious stones.

CONTRIBUTIONS

Ancient Mesopotamia is remembered for developing the first written language, writing some of the earliest known literature, and instituting the earliest known code of law. Mesopotamia is also noted for its ornate and complex art and architecture, a system of sewers and flush toilets, and the inventions of the wheel, plow, and sailboat. The Mesopotamians invented a math system based on the numeral 60, the earliest concepts of algebra and geometry, and a system of weights and measures that served the ancient world until the Roman period.

ANCIENT MESOPOTAMIA

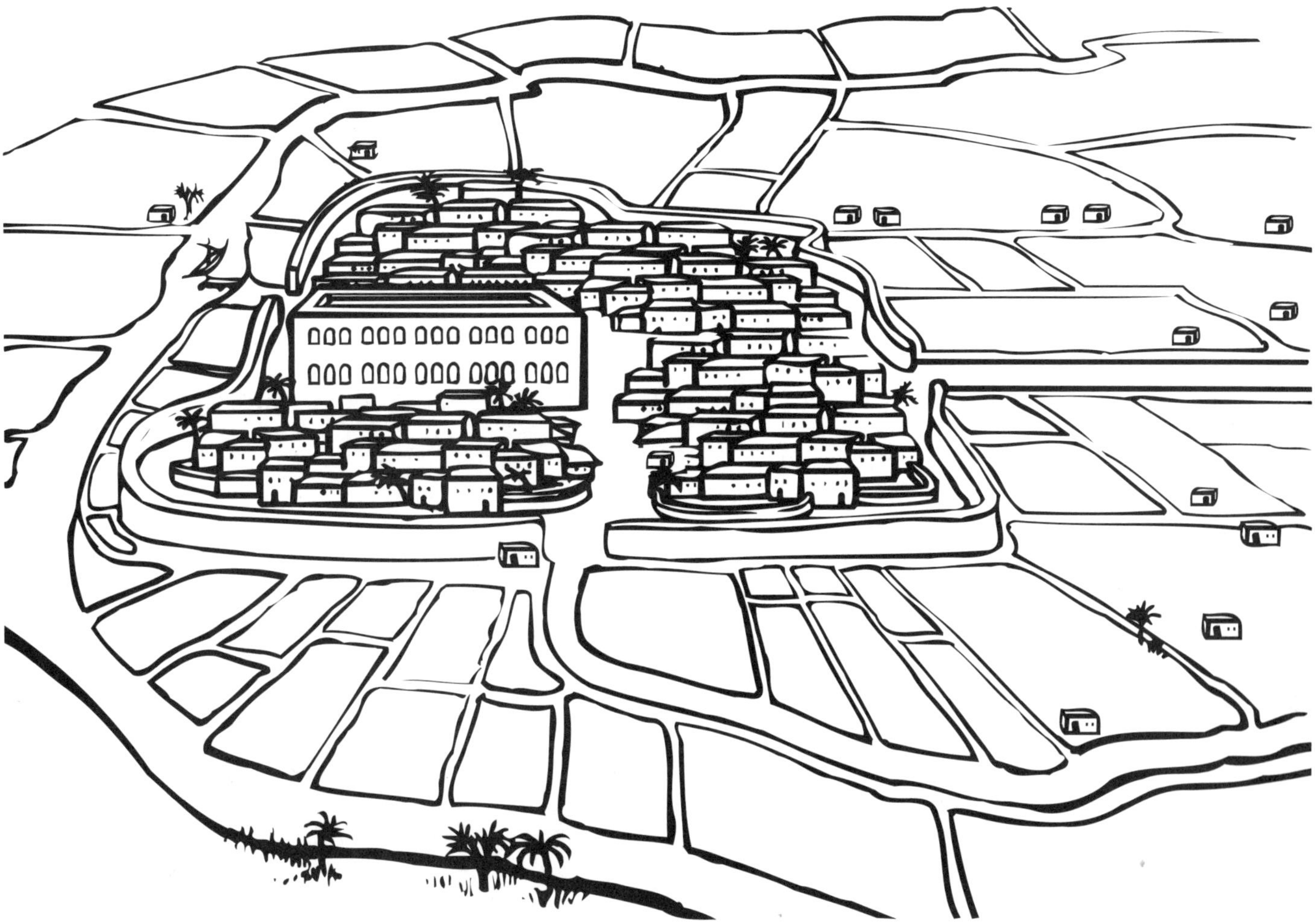

Mesopotamia was the land between the Tigris and the Euphrates Rivers. Mesopotamia was in the present-day countries of Iraq, Syria, and Turkey. The Mesopotamians built city-states. Each **city-state** had a big city and small villages around the city. There was also farmland in the city-state.

Farmers grew two **grains**. Those two grains were wheat and barley. The people liked to eat barley cakes and flatbread. They drank barley beer. Farmers raised cattle, sheep, goats, and pigs. The animals provided meat, milk, and butter. The people ate many vegetables such as cucumbers, peas, onions, and lettuce.

Houses in the city were made of sun-dried mud bricks. The houses were square or rectangular in shape. Most people lived in houses that were built around a central courtyard. Many two-story houses had balconies. They even had flush toilets. Poorer people lived in simple one-room houses.

Clothing was made from wool or **flax**. Men were bare-chested. Men wore skirts that tied at the waist. Women wore long gowns. The right arm and shoulder were left bare. Men and women wore wool shawls. Men and women wore gold and silver earrings and necklaces.

The Mesopotamians invented the first wheel and plow. They created the first map. The Mesopotamians made the first sailboat. They also built beautiful temples called **ziggurats**. The Mesopotamians were good inventors.

Note: Reproduce this page for each student. Follow the directions on page 17 to make this postcard.

POSTCARD FROM ANCIENT MESOPOTAMIA

The Hanging Gardens of Babylon were built by Nebuchadnezzar.

fold

Note: Reproduce this page for each student to use with the "Mesopotamian Puppets" activity, as described on page 18.

MESOPOTAMIAN PUPPETS

MATERIALS

- page 27, reproduced for each student
- page 28, reproduced, one sailboat for each student
- 9" x 12" (23 x 30.5 cm) blue construction paper
- construction paper scraps
- crayons or marking pens
- craft stick
- craft knife
- scissors
- glue

SAILING ON THE RIVER

After a discussion of the importance of the Tigris and Euphrates Rivers to travel and trade in Mesopotamia, students make this model of a Mesopotamian boat and sail it down the Tigris River.

STEPS TO FOLLOW

1. Read and discuss the map and information on pages 27 and 28.
2. Have students color and glue their maps onto the construction paper.
3. Have a helper carefully cut a slit between the dotted lines on the Tigris River.
4. Guide students through the following steps to make the boat:
   a. Color and cut out the boat pattern. Glue it to construction paper and cut around it.
   b. Glue the boat to the top of a craft stick.
   c. From the back of the page, slip the boat up through the river slit, facing the front.
5. Have students "sail" their boats on the river.

SAILING ON THE RIVER

The Mesopotamians were the first to use sailboats. They used sailboats to travel on the Euphrates and Tigris Rivers. The mountain people had wood, gold, silver, and copper. They traded those things to get wheat and barley. The sailboats carried those things to the people in Mesopotamia. The sailboats helped everybody get what they needed.

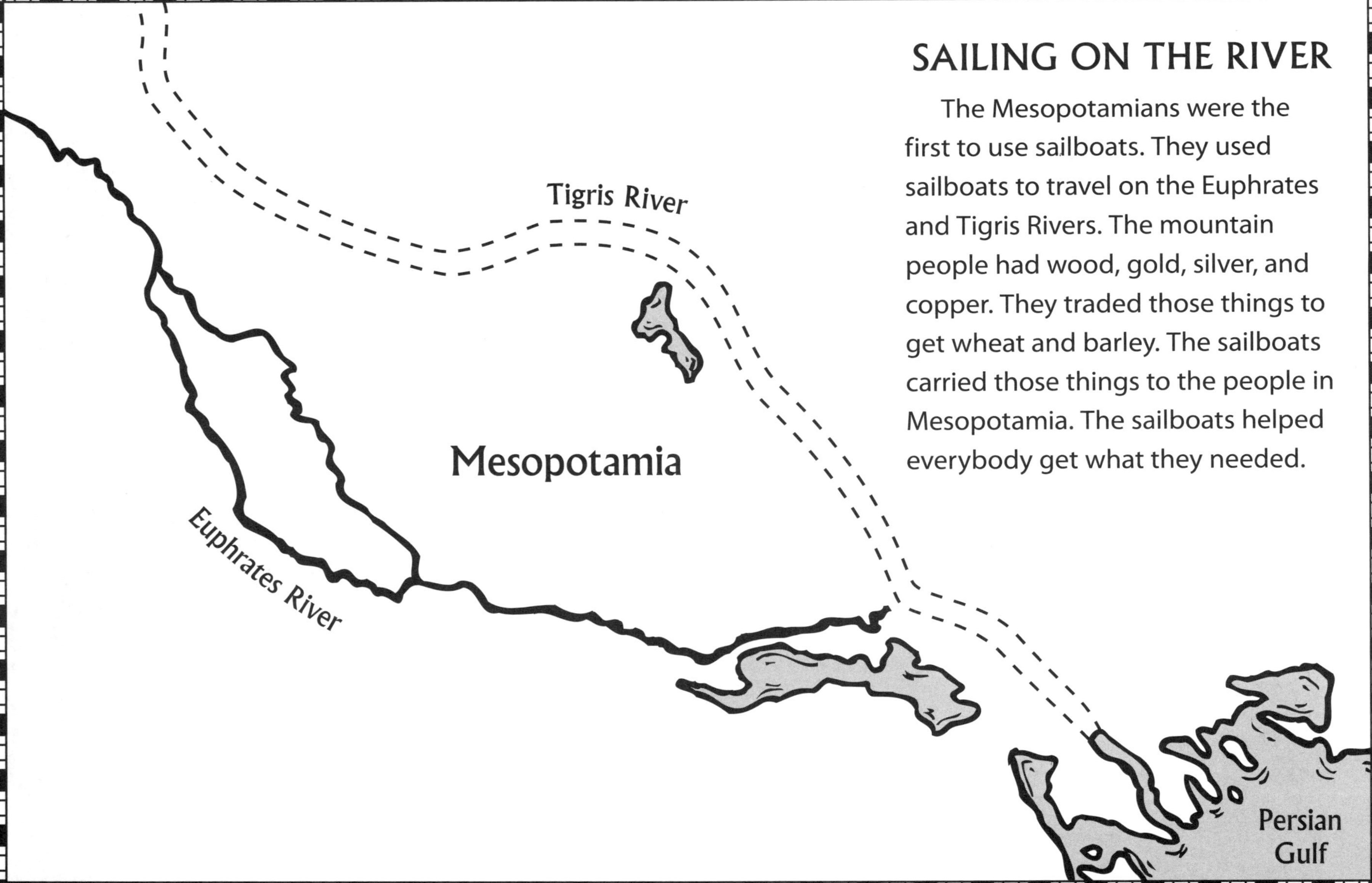

SAILING ON THE RIVER

ZIGGURAT POP-UP BOOK

Students learn about the temple called a ziggurat when they make a pop-up book.

STEPS TO FOLLOW

1. Read the information about the ziggurat on page 30. Tell students they are going to make a pop-up model of the ziggurat.
2. Guide students through the following steps to create the pop-up:
   a. Cut out the pattern for the pop-up on page 30.
   b. Fold the card in half and cut the tab as shown.
   c. Fold and crease the tab in both directions.
   d. Open the card and pull the tab forward.

2b.

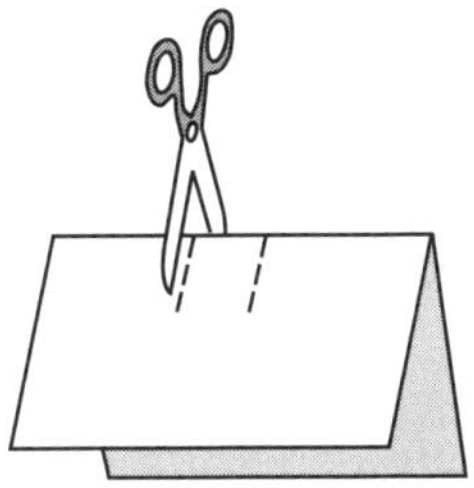

2c.

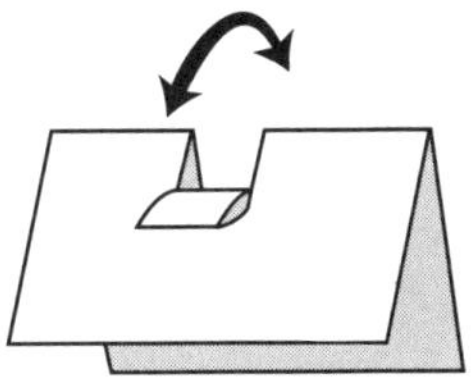

3. Direct students to color and cut out the ziggurat pattern.
4. Have students glue the ziggurat to the tab on the pop-up.
5. Fold the construction paper in half. Glue the pop-up inside as shown.

Place glue on the pop-up, close the folder, and press firmly. Flip the book over and follow the same steps in gluing the back.

6. You may want students to color a scene behind the ziggurat.

MATERIALS

- page 30, reproduced for each student
- page 31, reproduced, one ziggurat for each student
- 9″ x 12″ (23 x 30.5 cm) construction paper
- crayons or marking pens
- scissors
- glue

ZIGGURAT POP-UP BOOK PATTERN

fold

fold

fold

fold

THE ZIGGURAT

Every city in Mesopotamia had a temple. The temple was called a ziggurat. The temple was the largest and most important building. It was located in the center of the city. The ziggurat was where people went to worship their gods and goddesses.

The ziggurat was built on top of a mud-brick platform. The ziggurat could be three to seven stories high. There were stairs and ramps to get to each level. As the people climbed higher up the stairs, they thought they were getting closer to the gods. There were many storerooms in the temple where priests worked. A one-room shrine was on top. The shrine looked like a crown.

ZIGGURAT POP-UP BOOK PATTERN

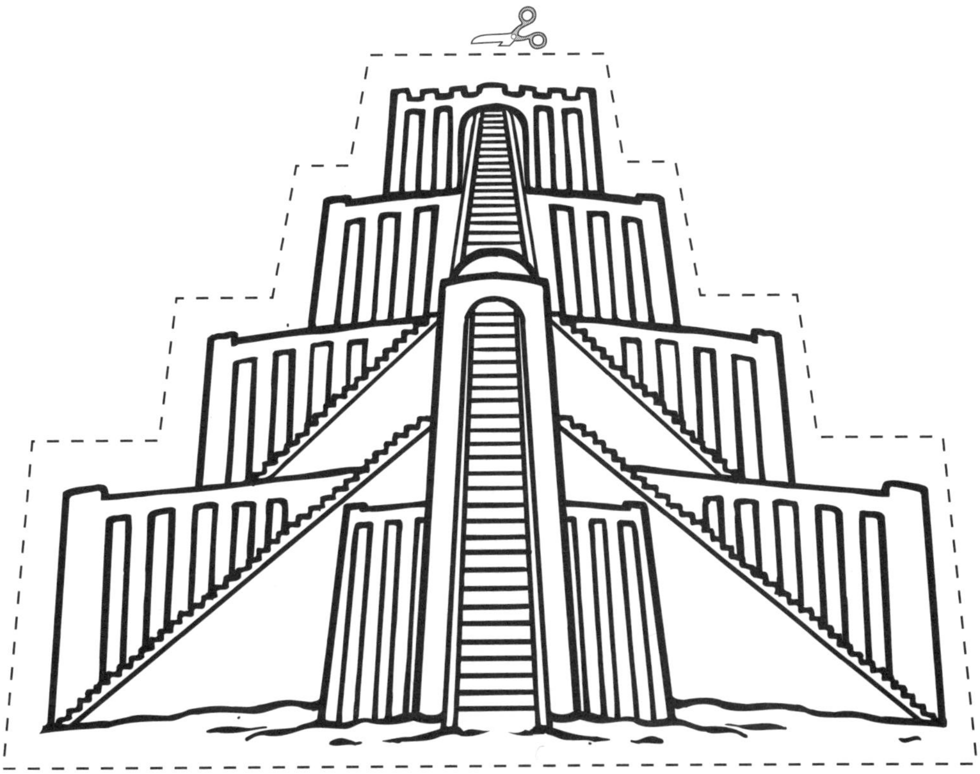

Pocket 3

ANCIENT EGYPT

CUT AND PASTE

Pocket Label, Words to Know .... **page 33**
See page 2 for information on how to prepare the pocket label. See page 10 for information on how to prepare the "Words to Know" activity.

FACT SHEET

Ancient Egypt .... **page 34**
Read this background information to familiarize yourself with the ancient civilization of Egypt. Share the information with your students as appropriate. Incorporate library and multimedia resources that are available.

STUDENT BOOKLET

Make an Ancient Egypt Booklet .... **pages 35–37**
See page 2 for information on how to prepare the student booklet. Read and discuss the information booklet as a class. Encourage students to read their booklets to partners or independently.

ACTIVITIES

Postcard from Ancient Egypt .... **page 38**
Students pretend they have visited ancient Egypt and "send" this postcard to a friend. Follow the directions on page 17 for making this postcard.

Egyptian Puppets .... **page 39**
Students color and cut out the puppets showing typical Egyptian clothing. Mount the puppets on construction paper, and then attach them to craft sticks. Allow students to use the puppets to retell the story of ancient Egypt.

Life Along the Nile .... **pages 40 & 41**
A crocodile gives the students a tour of the important Nile River.

The Great Pyramid .... **pages 42 & 43**
This fold-up model is filled with fascinating facts about this amazing structure. Students cut out the shape and fold the sides to create a pyramid.

WORDS TO KNOW

See page 10 for directions.

hieroglyphics

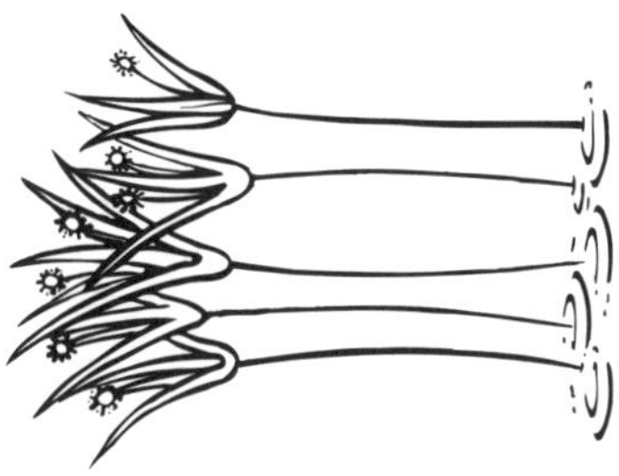

papyrus

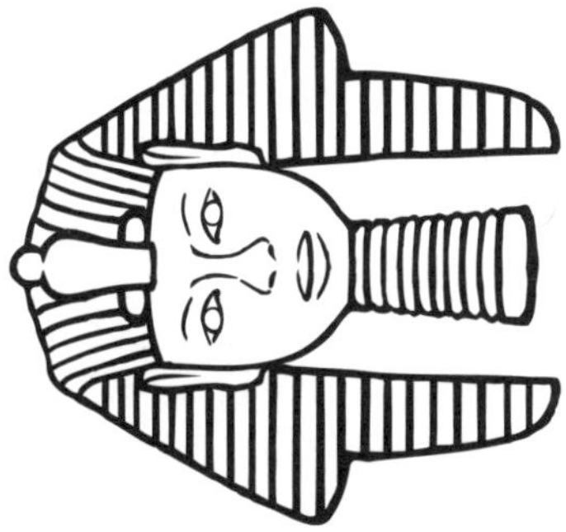

pharaoh

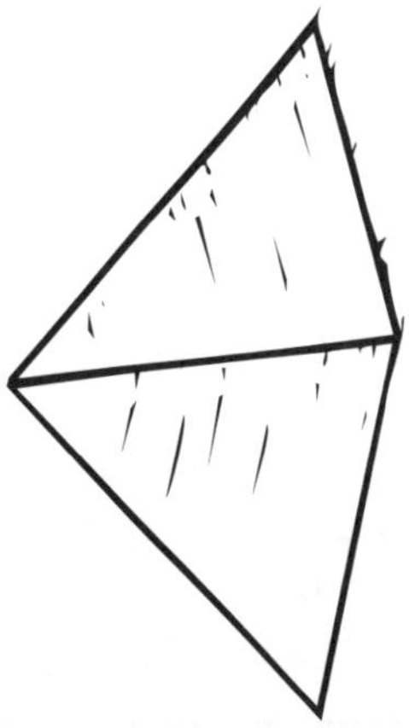

pyramid

FACT SHEET

ANCIENT EGYPT

The ancient Egyptian civilization lasted for roughly 3,000 years. Egyptian history is usually divided into three periods or kingdoms: Old Kingdom—2686 B.C. to 2186 B.C.; Middle Kingdom—2055 B.C. to 1650 B.C.; and New Kingdom—1550 B.C. to 1069 B.C.

Kings called pharaohs ruled ancient Egypt. The Egyptians believed each new pharaoh was the god Horus in human form. The pharaohs had supreme power and ruled the wealthiest kingdom of the ancient world.

The Nile River was called Egypt's lifeline. Every year the Nile flooded and deposited rich black soil along the banks. The fertile soil allowed the Egyptians to raise a surplus of food. The Nile River provided water for irrigation and it was a major transportation route. The ancient Egyptians fished and hunted animals such as Nile perch, ducks, cranes, ibis, hippopotamuses, and crocodiles. Papyrus, a long, thin reed, grew along the banks of the Nile. The papyrus reed was made into paper.

Religion was an important part of Egyptian life. The ancient Egyptians believed that gods and goddesses influenced every part of daily life. They also believed in the afterlife. This belief in the afterlife led the ancient Egyptians to construct pyramids and other great tombs for the pharaohs. They believed that the bodies of the dead should be mummified and then placed in coffins to preserve the body in the afterlife.

FOOD

The staple for the common Egyptian diet was bread. Poor Egyptians added beer, vegetables, and fish. Garlic and onions were popular seasonings. The wealthy consumed such delicacies as goose, roast beef, pomegranates, figs, and wine.

SHELTER

The majority of Egyptians lived in towns and villages along the Nile Valley. Because of the yearly flooding, they built their houses on the edge of the desert or on patches of high ground. The houses were built from dried mud bricks and covered with a white limestone plaster to deflect the heat of the sun. A shelter was built on the roof to catch cool north breezes. In hot weather, families spent most of their time on the roof.

Rich Egyptians had bathrooms. To take a shower, a servant poured water over the bather who stood on a stone slab. Toilets were stone seats with a hole. Underneath the hole was a large sand-filled urn that was changed from time to time.

CLOTHING

Egyptians wore lightweight clothing made from fine linen cloth. The cloth was draped around the body. No one wore underwear.

The basic woman's dress—a simple tube made from a rectangle of linen sewn down one side, with straps attached to the top edge—remained the same throughout the three kingdoms. During the Middle Kingdom, some women added a colorful collar. During the New Kingdom, a pleated, fringed robe was worn over the dress.

Men wore knee-length kilts during the Old Kingdom. The linen cloth was pleated and fastened at the waist with a knot or a buckle. In the Middle Kingdom, the style of kilts changed. They were longer and straighter.

Boys' heads were shaved except for one long braided lock that hung at the side. Many Egyptians wore wigs for special occasions. Men and women wore makeup, perfumed oils, and jewelry.

CONTRIBUTIONS

The ancient Egyptians made many contributions to the development of civilizations. They built the great Pyramids. The Pyramids at Giza were enormous stone pyramids that still stand today. The ancient Egyptians created the 365-day calendar and invented a form of picture writing called hieroglyphics. They also invented a kind of paper made from the stems of papyrus plants. Their tomb paintings and enormous stone statues represented fine art and architecture. Art objects and jewelry made from materials such as gold and alabaster were valued greatly.

ANCIENT EGYPT

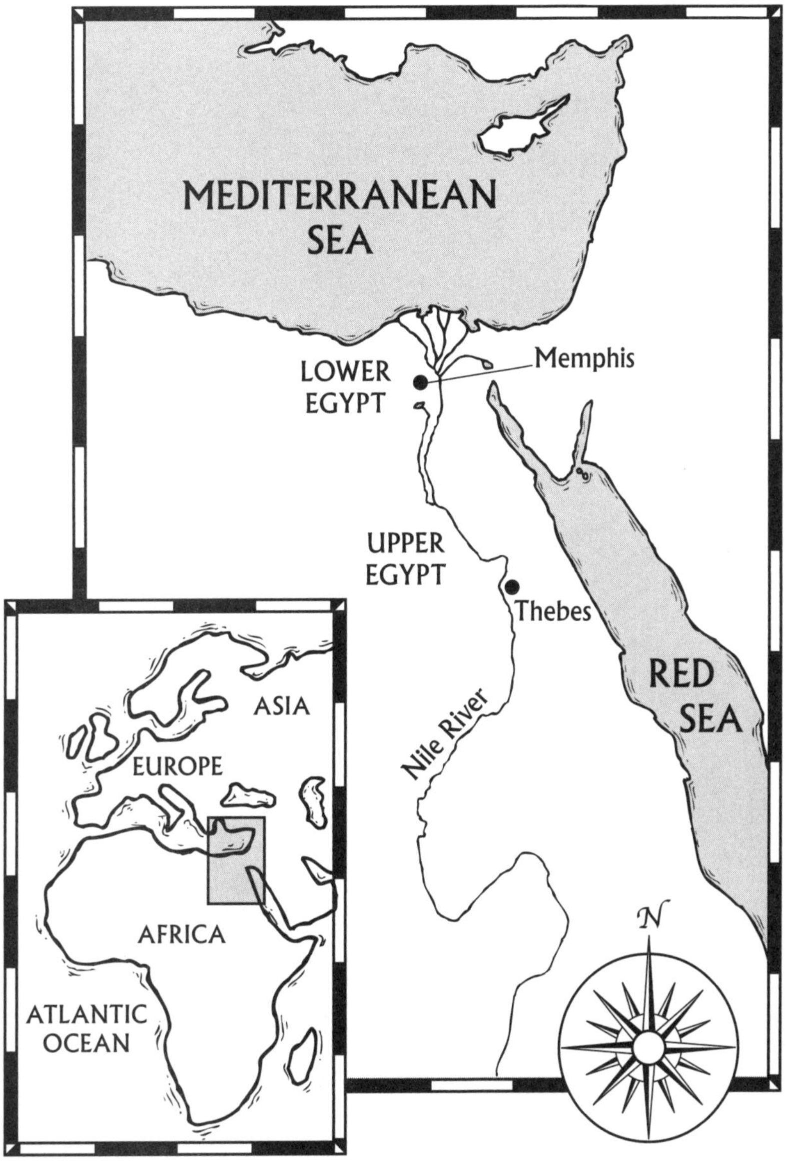

The first Egyptians settled in the Nile River Valley. That was over 5,000 years ago. People grew crops in the rich soil beside the Nile River. The river valley was surrounded by desert. The desert helped keep invaders away. The desert had sandstone and limestone for building pyramids. There was also gold in the desert for making jewelry.

Egyptians ate lots of bread. They ate onions, peas, and beans. They liked fruit such as pomegranates, figs, and dates. They ate fish from the Nile River. Egyptians drank barley beer and wine. Cooking was done outside or on the rooftop. Egyptians sat at low tables and ate with their fingers.

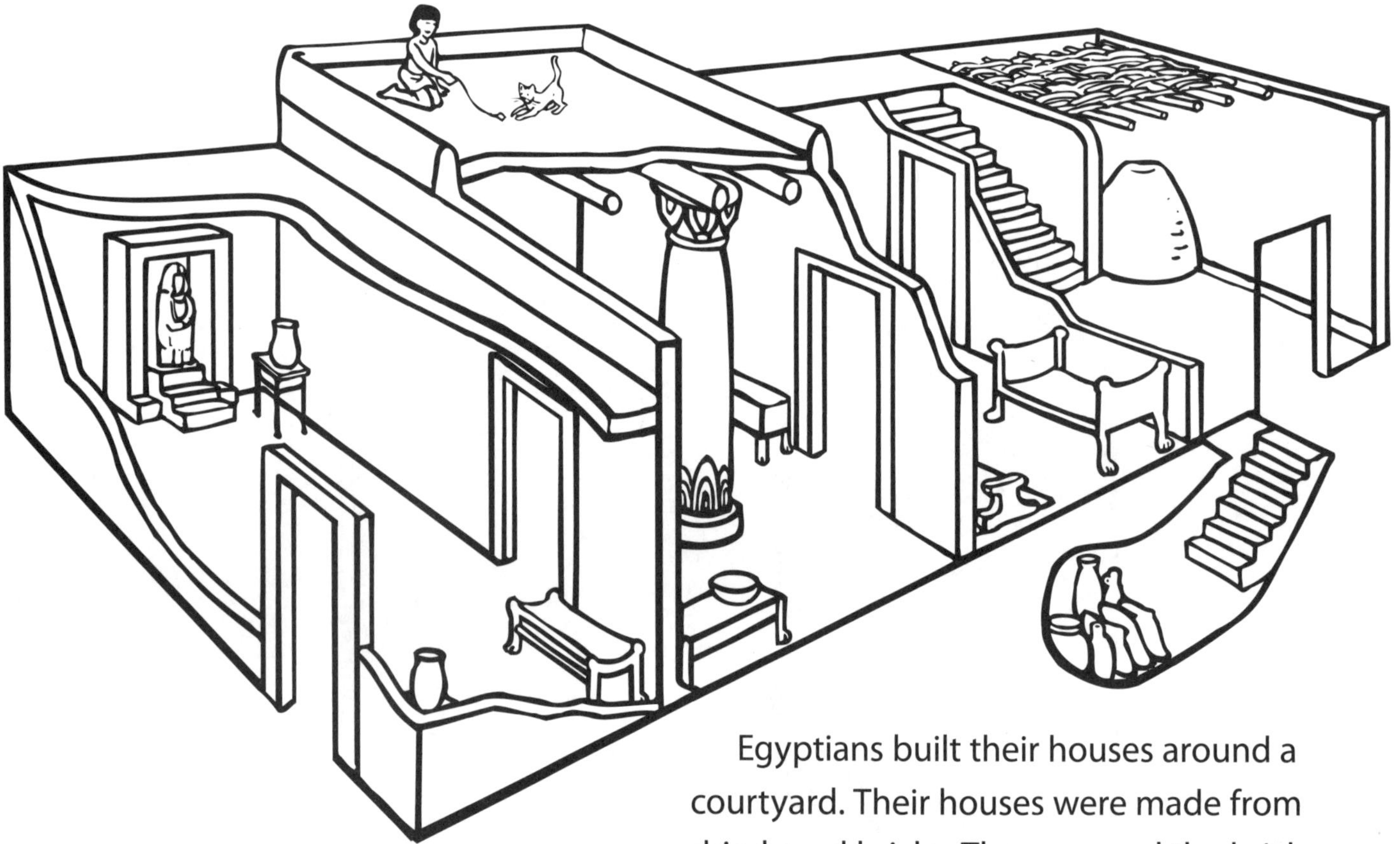

Egyptians built their houses around a courtyard. Their houses were made from dried mud bricks. They covered the bricks with white limestone plaster. Most houses had three or four small rooms. The houses had small, high windows. This made the house dark even in the daytime. In hot weather, families spent most of their time on the roof.

Egyptian clothing was light and cool. Women wore simple dresses made from a rectangle of linen. They tied the rectangle together with a knot. This made a shawl. Men wore short skirts knotted or pinned at the waist. Both men and women wore makeup, jewelry, and perfumed oils.

People remember the ancient Egyptians. They built the great **Pyramids**. The Egyptians made huge statues such as the Sphinx. They used picture writing called **hieroglyphics**. The Egyptians invented **papyrus**. This was paper made from the stems of papyrus plants. The Egyptians had leaders called **pharaohs**.

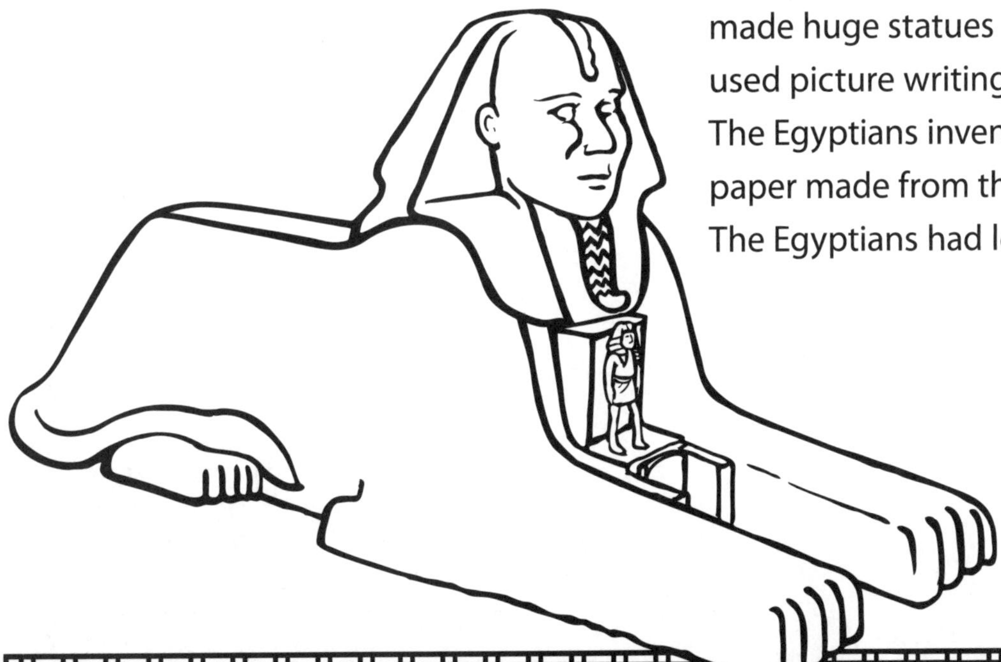

Note: Reproduce this page for each student. Follow the directions on page 17 to make this postcard.

POSTCARD FROM ANCIENT EGYPT

**The Great Pyramid was built to honor Pharaoh Khufu.
It stands alongside two other pyramids near Giza, Egypt.**

fold

Note: Reproduce this page for each student to use with the "Egyptian Puppets" activity, as described on page 32.

EGYPTIAN PUPPETS

LIFE ALONG THE NILE

The Nile River was vital to the ancient Egyptians. Not only did this long river provide rich soil and papyrus plants, it was home to a large variety of animals.

Students take a trip down the Nile to learn about all the life that flourished on this great river.

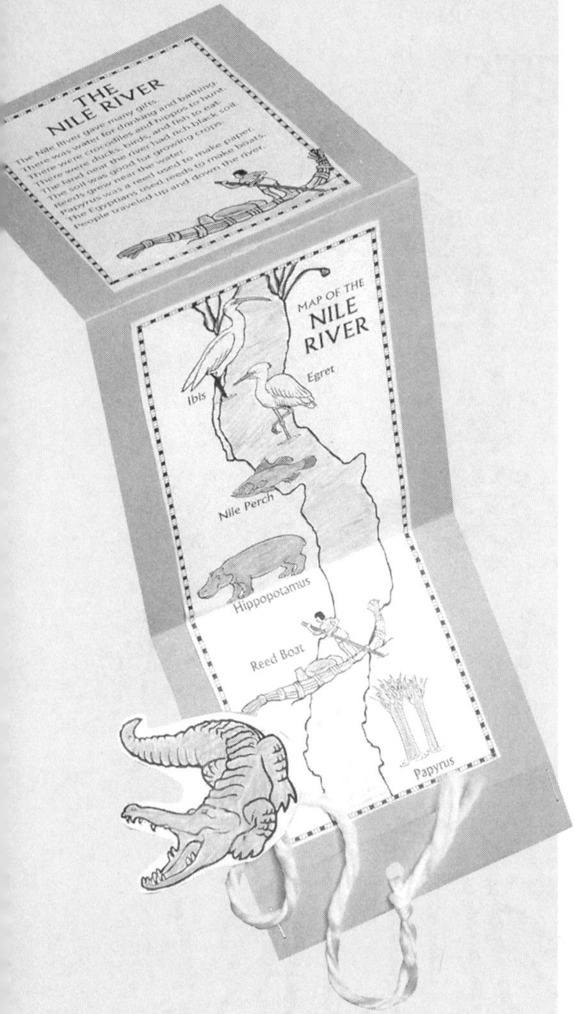

MATERIALS

- page 41, reproduced for each student
- 5″ x 18″ (13 x 45.5 cm) construction paper
- 4″ x 6″ (10 x 15 cm) construction paper
- 15″ (38 cm) yarn
- scissors
- stapler
- hole punch
- glue
- crayons

STEPS TO FOLLOW

1. Discuss the information about the importance of the Nile River with students.
2. Have students color and cut out the crocodile, the information about the Nile River, and the map of the Nile River.
3. Direct students to glue the crocodile to the smaller piece of construction paper and cut around the shape, leaving a thin border.
4. Have students accordion-fold the larger piece of construction paper into thirds as shown.
5. Direct students to fold up the bottom of the paper 1″ (2.5 cm) and staple, making a flap for the crocodile to sit in.
6. Have students glue the information to the top third of the paper. Then instruct them to glue the map onto the rest of the paper.
7. Help students punch a hole in the flap at the bottom of the paper. Then have them tie one end of the yarn to the hole. Staple the crocodile to the other end of the yarn.
8. Instruct students to use the crocodile as a tour guide of the Nile River. Store the crocodile in the flap.

Steps 4 through 8

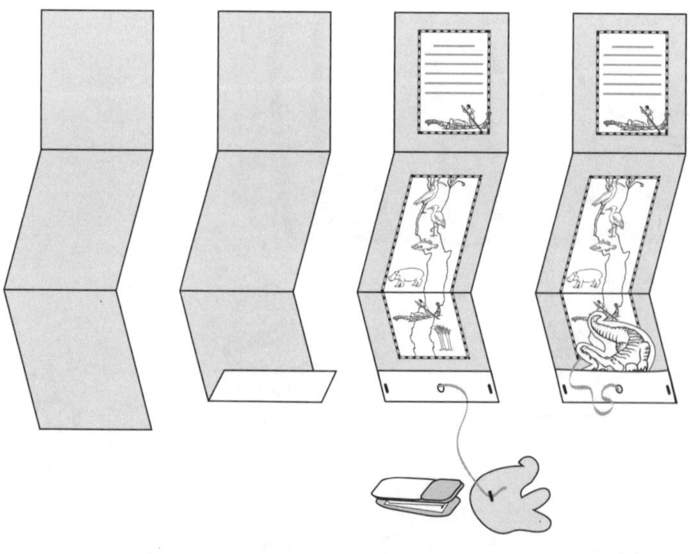

PATTERNS FOR LIFE ALONG THE NILE

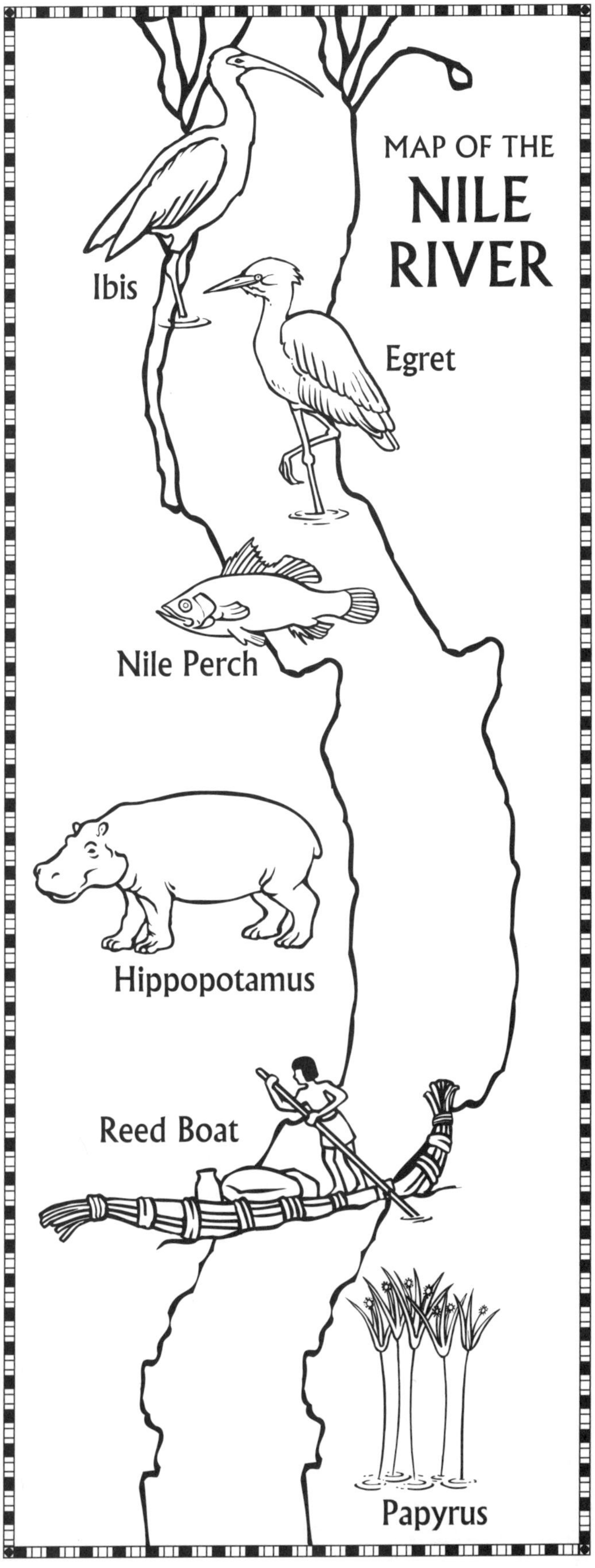

THE NILE RIVER

The Nile River gave many gifts.
There was water for drinking and bathing.
There were crocodiles and hippos to hunt.
There were ducks, birds, and fish to eat.
The land near the river had rich black soil.
The soil was good for growing crops.
Reeds grew near the water.
Papyrus was a reed used to make paper.
The Egyptians used reeds to make boats.
People traveled up and down the river.

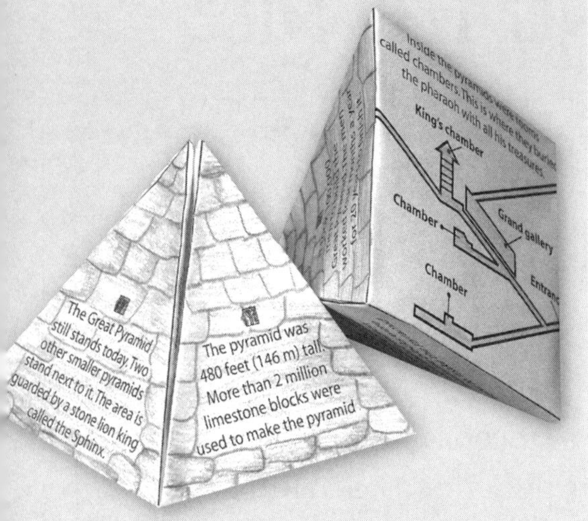

THE GREAT PYRAMID

The largest of the pyramids built at Giza was the Great Pyramid. It was built for King Khufu. The Great Pyramid was originally 480 feet (146 m) tall. It contained more than 2 million stone blocks that averaged 2½ short tons (2.3 metric tonnes) each. The base of the pyramid was about 13 acres (5 hectares).

The ancient Egyptians used no machines or iron tools. They cut the limestone blocks using copper chisels and saws. They built long ramps and dragged the stones up as they built each new layer. After all the blocks were in place, men carefully covered them with white casing stones. They polished the stones to make them shine.

Today, the Great Pyramid still stands at Giza. Some of the upper stones are gone, so it now stands 450 feet (137 m) tall. The Great Pyramid is one of the three pyramids at the site that millions of tourists visit yearly. The Pyramids at Giza are the only remaining wonder of the Seven Wonders of the Ancient World.

Students learn about the Great Pyramid when they make their own pyramid of facts.

MATERIALS

- page 43, reproduced for each student
- crayons
- scissors

STEPS TO FOLLOW

1. Show a picture of the Great Pyramid at Giza as you discuss the facts about it with students.
2. Have students read the facts on the pyramid pattern.
3. Direct students to cut out the pyramid pattern.
4. Students then turn the pyramid over and draw blocks of stone.
5. Have students fold on the lines to make the pyramid stand up. The pyramid is not glued together so that it can be folded to fit into the pocket.

THE GREAT PYRAMID

fold under

fold under

fold under

fold under

fold under

fold under

fold under

fold under

The Great Pyramid was built 4,500 years ago for King Khufu.

The Great Pyramid still stands today. Two other smaller pyramids stand next to it. The area is guarded by a stone lion king called the Sphinx.

Inside the pyramids were rooms called chambers. This is where they buried the pharaoh with all his treasures.

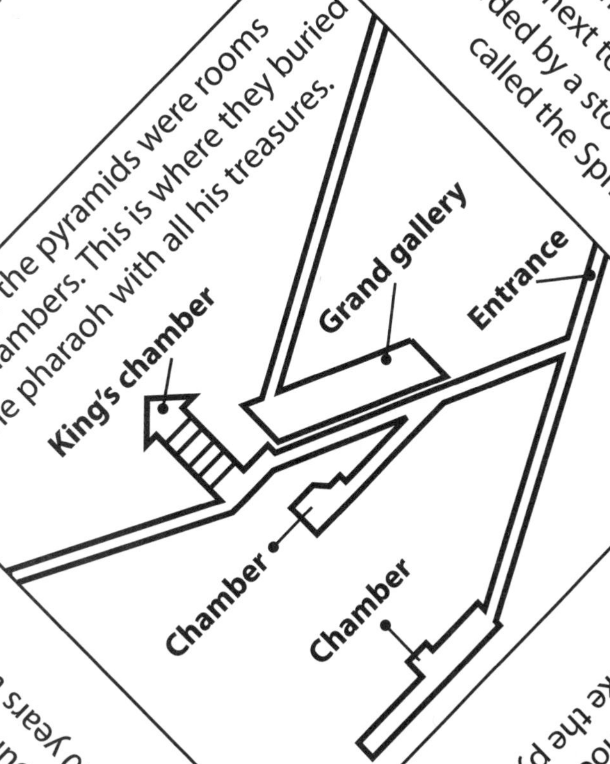

It took 100,000 men to build the Great Pyramid. The men worked four months a year for 20 years to finish it.

The pyramid was 480 feet (146 m) tall. More than 2 million limestone blocks were used to make the pyramid.

Pocket 4

ANCIENT GREECE

CUT AND PASTE

Pocket Label, Words to Know............... **page 45**
See page 2 for information on how to prepare the pocket label. See page 10 for information on how to prepare the "Words to Know" activity.

FACT SHEET

Ancient Greece............................. **page 46**
Use this page as a quick reference for facts about ancient Greece. For more detailed information, use library and Internet resources.

STUDENT BOOKLET

Make an Ancient Greece Booklet...... **pages 47–49**
See page 2 for information on how to prepare the student booklet. Read and discuss the information booklet as a class. Encourage students to read their booklets to partners or independently.

ACTIVITIES

Postcard from Ancient Greece.............. **page 50**
Students pretend they have visited ancient Greece and "send" this postcard to a friend. Follow the directions on page 17 for making this postcard.

Grecian Puppets .... **page 51**
Students color and cut out the puppets showing Grecian clothing. Mount the puppets on construction paper, and then attach them to craft sticks. Allow students to use the puppets to retell the story of ancient Greece.

The Parthenon Shape Book .... **pages 52–54**
The Parthenon was a beautiful temple built to honor the goddess Athena. Students learn about this temple when they make a double-hinged book of the Parthenon.

Theater Mask.. **pages 55–57**
Greek actors showed the comedic and tragic sides of their characters. Students make a two-sided mask, showing both a happy and a sad face.

WORDS TO KNOW

See page 10 for directions.

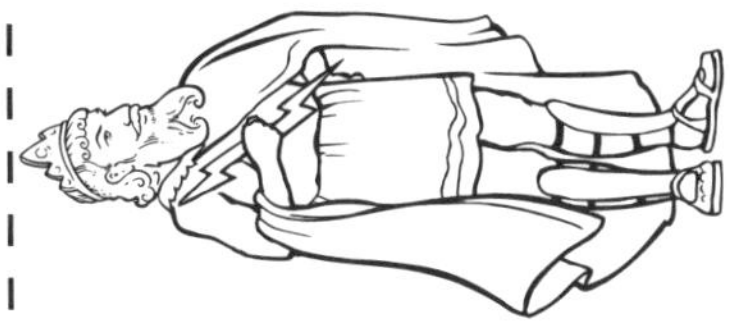

myth

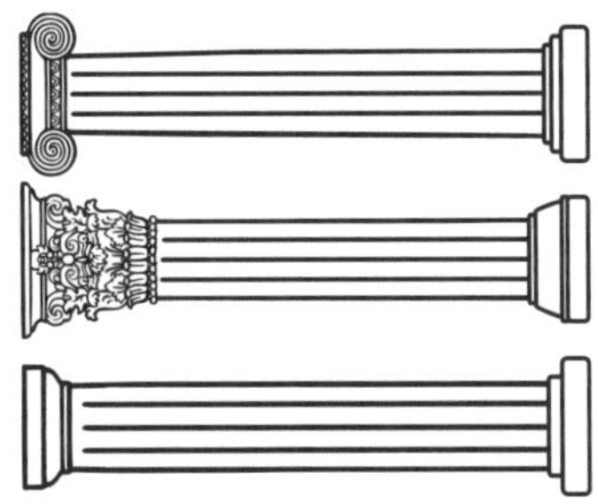

columns

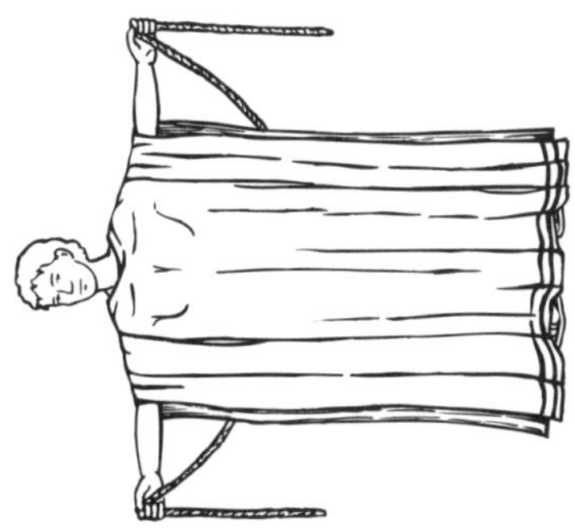

chiton

agora

FACT SHEET
ANCIENT GREECE

The lands of the ancient Greeks were islands and peninsulas bordering the Aegean Sea. The Aegean Sea was the crossroads of the ancient Mediterranean world. The Greek countryside was mountainous, making land travel hard, but traders, explorers, and adventurers all passed through the islands. The people who settled there formed a single culture. They called it "Hellas." It began about the same time as the Bronze Age in 3500 B.C.

Ancient Greeks lived in city-states. The Greek city-state was a small, self-governing city and the surrounding countryside. There were several hundred city-states in ancient Greece.

The ancient Greeks worshiped many gods. They believed that the gods and goddesses controlled all things. Greek gods were related to each other and had human behaviors, but were more powerful than humans. Greek writers wrote myths explaining life and nature, using the gods and goddesses as characters.

Greeks were skilled sailors, accomplished architects, builders, musicians, playwrights, actors, philosophers, politicians, artists, poets, and soldiers.

FOOD

Greek children most often ate crusty bread, vegetables, and fish along with goat cheese, olives, fruits, and nuts. Meat was a rare treat that was only available on holidays. Children ate with a knife and spoon. They drank water, goat's milk, and occasionally watered-down wine. Usually men dined only with men and women dined only with other women and their children. Only at special festivals did men and women dine together.

A special dinner began with a plate of fresh, tasty cold foods called meze. This might include pita bread, feta cheese, olives, and hummus, a spread made from chickpeas.

SHELTER

Greek homes had stone foundations, mud-brick walls, and pottery-tile roofs. The small, high windows were covered with shutters. The house was built around an open courtyard. In the courtyard there was a well and an altar where members of a Greek family worshiped the gods.

CLOTHING

The ancient Greeks wore simple clothes made from linen or wool. Boys and men wore a straight tunic called a chiton. It ended at the knee and was pinned at the shoulders and belted at the waist. The chiton was worn so that it covered only one shoulder, leaving the other bare. Girls and women wore ankle-length chitons.

Both men and women wore woolen cloaks called himations. Ancient Greeks usually went barefoot or wore sandals. For exercising and playing sports, men wore no clothes, and women wore a short chiton or nothing at all.

CONTRIBUTIONS

The influence of Greek architecture, art, literature, history, philosophy, science, and mathematics can be seen throughout the world. The ancient Greeks designed the Doric, Ionic, and Corinthian columns. In literature, epic and lyric poetry was perfected by the Greeks. Greek tragedies and comedies began in ancient Greece. They built large open-air theaters that could seat over 10,000 people.

The ancient Greeks had many great philosophers, historians, mathematicians, and scientists. Best known of the philosophers were Socrates, Plato, and Aristotle. Herodotus was called the "father of history." Pythagorus and Euclid made great strides in geometry. Hippocrates was a famous doctor.

The ancient Greeks believed in a strong mind and body. They had the first Olympics to honor the gods. Each city-state sent their best athletes to compete in discus and javelin throwing, jumping, wrestling, and running.

In addition to all these contributions, the Greeks' ideas about democracy and government have had an important influence on modern societies.

ANCIENT GREECE

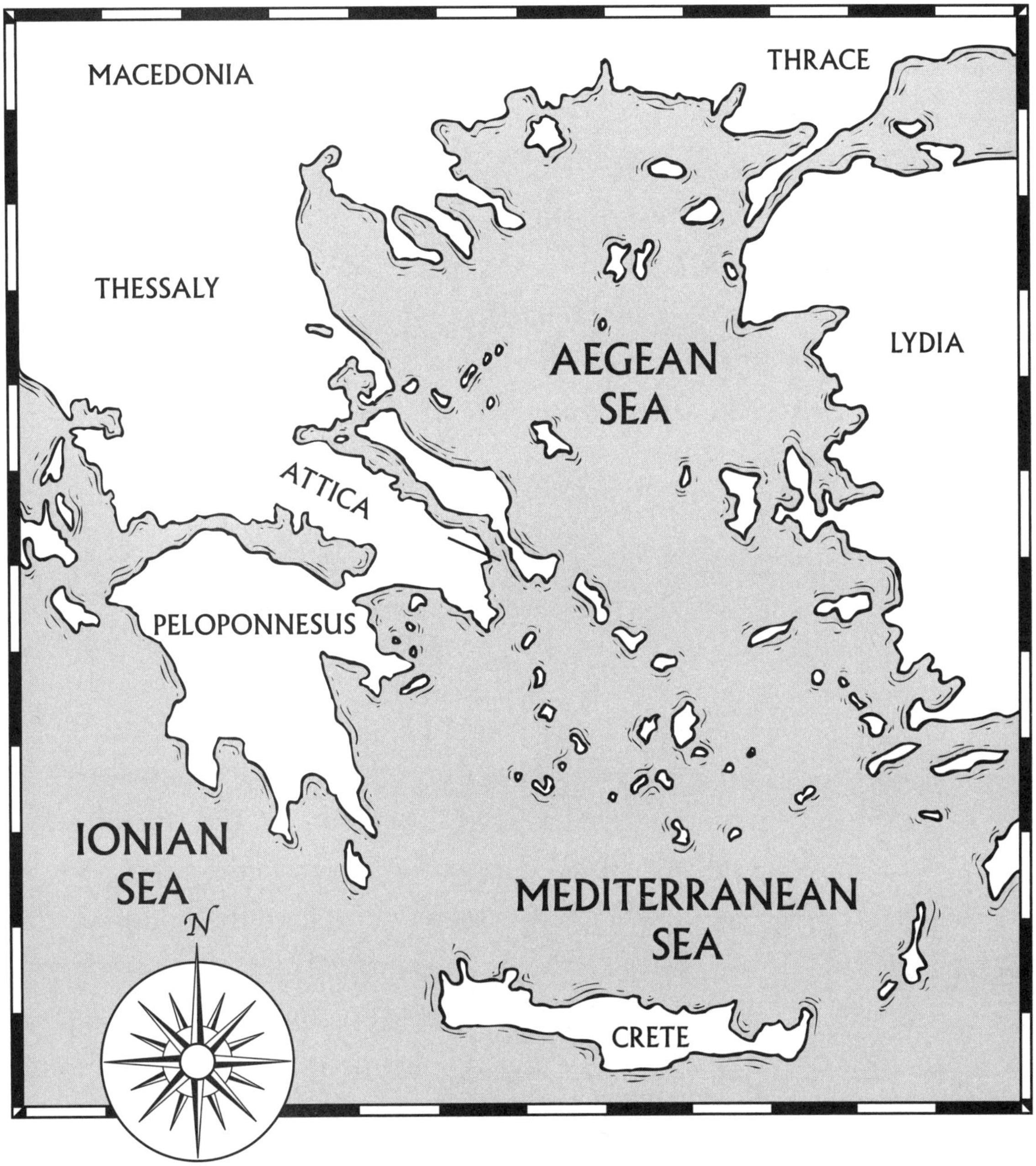

In 3500 B.C., people came to the islands of the Aegean Sea. They built a large civilization on the islands and on the mainland of Greece. The two most famous cities were called Athens and Sparta. Greece has lots of mountains. The biggest mountain is called Mount Olympus.

Most people were farmers. They grew wheat and barley for bread and porridge. They got fish, sea urchins, octopus, and squid from the sea. The Greeks drank goat's milk and wine. People went to the agora to buy their favorite foods. The **agora** was a big marketplace. They liked to buy foods such olives, figs, and grapes.

Greek houses were one- or two-story homes. They were built around a courtyard. Homes were made of mud bricks. They had clay tile roofs. The kitchen and bathroom were on the first floor. Men entertained their guests there, too. The family bedrooms, the servants' room, and the women's weaving room were upstairs.

People wore wool or linen tunics called **chitons**. Women wore long one- or two-piece chitons. Men wore thigh-length chitons. During the winter, people wore cloaks called himations. For exercising and playing sports, men wore no clothes. People wore leather sandals outside. They went barefoot inside the house.

The ancient Greeks had the first Olympics. They gave plays in large outdoor theaters. Greek writers made up stories about the gods and goddesses. They are called **myths**. The Greeks made three types of **columns** for buildings. They are called Doric, Ionic, and Corinthian. The Greeks built a beautiful temple called the Parthenon.

Note: Reproduce this page for each student. Follow the directions on page 17 to make this postcard.

POSTCARD FROM ANCIENT GREECE

The Parthenon was built as a temple to honor the goddess Athena.

fold

Note: Reproduce this page for each student to use with the "Grecian Puppets" activity, as described on page 44.

GRECIAN PUPPETS

MATERIALS

- pages 53 and 54, reproduced for each student
- 9" x 18" (23 x 45.5 cm) construction paper
- pencil
- crayons or marking pens
- scissors
- glue

THE PARTHENON SHAPE BOOK

Students make a book about the greatest temple of ancient Greece.

STEPS TO FOLLOW

1. Before the lesson, cut a construction paper Parthenon for each student as shown.
2. Have students color and cut out the patterns.
3. Direct students to open up the Parthenon and glue the statue of Athena in the center panel. Have students write the title "The Parthenon" above the statue.
4. Then students glue the Athena fact boxes on either side of the statue.
5. Direct students to glue fact boxes about the Parthenon on each side panel.
6. Allow to dry.
7. Instruct students to fold the sides to the center and glue the column "doors" to each outside panel as shown.
8. Now they can open up the column doors of the Parthenon to see Athena and read the facts about the Parthenon.

Steps 1 & 7

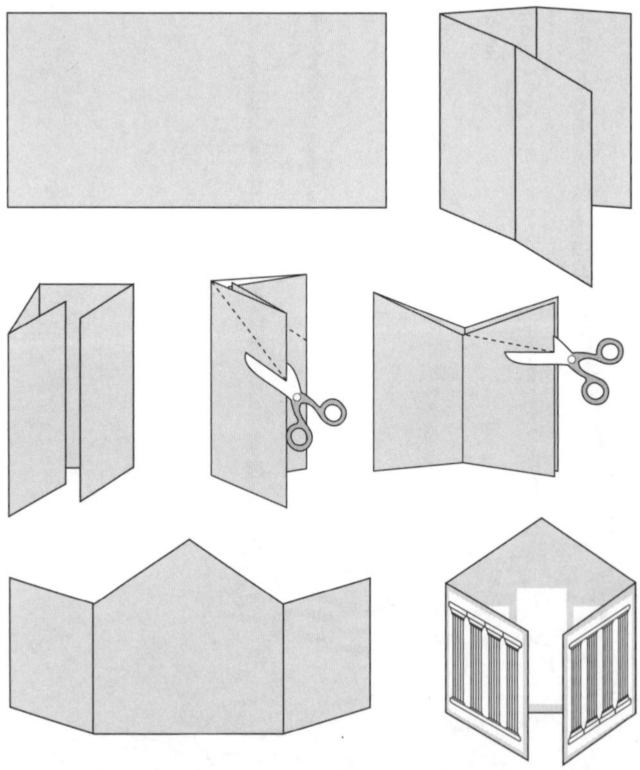

ATHENA

Inside the Parthenon was a statue of Athena. Athena was the goddess of wisdom and war. The statue of Athena was 40 feet (12 m) tall. She was made of gold and ivory.

Athena wore a helmet and carried a shield. The gold shield had a snake on it. She held a small winged statue of Nike. Nike was the goddess of victory.

The Parthenon was a great marble temple. It was built for the goddess Athena. The Parthenon is in ruins today. People still go to Athens to see the Parthenon.

The Parthenon was 60 feet (18 m) tall. It had 46 Doric columns. On the top were painted carvings. Most carvings were of men on horseback.

THE PARTHENON

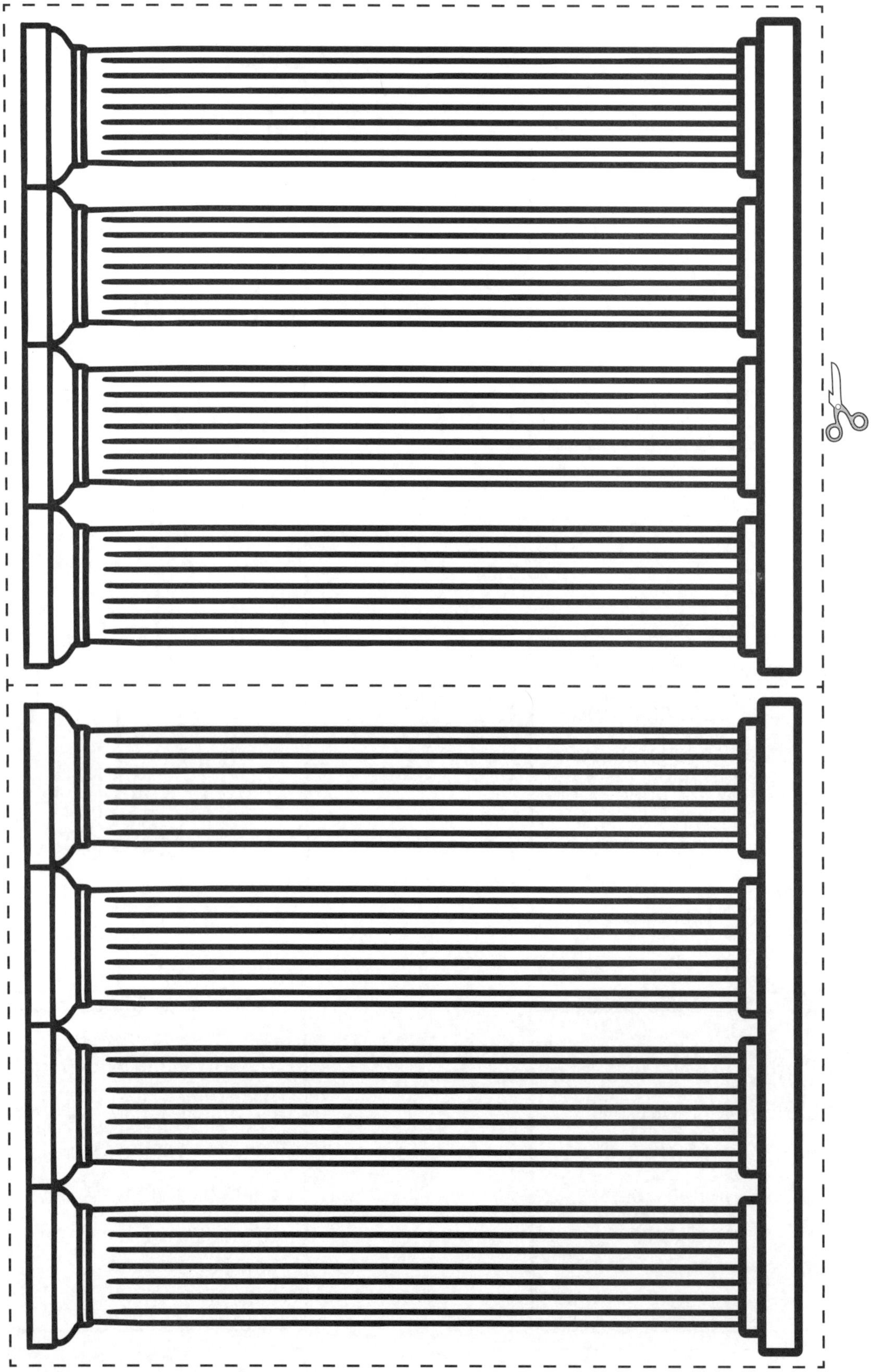

THEATER MASK

Greek actors performed both comedies and tragedies in large open-air theaters. Actors wore masks to represent different people and emotions. The actors were all males, so they had to play female parts also. The masks had large openings for the mouth and eyes. Some actors wore two masks at the same time. One was over the face and the other was worn on the back of the head. That way they could quickly switch characters or show two different emotions.

Students make a two-sided mask to show both a happy and a sad face.

STEPS TO FOLLOW

1. Discuss theater in ancient Greece and explain how masks were worn.
2. Have students color and cut out the two masks on pages 56 and 57.
3. Help students cut out the eyes and mouth for each mask.
4. Make a headband out of the construction paper strip to fit the student's head.
5. Staple masks to the front and back of the headband.
6. Have students put on the masks with the happy side showing in front. Ask students to tell a happy story to a partner, and then do the same with the sad side of the mask.
7. To store the masks in the pocket, tell students to gently fold the headband.

MATERIALS

- pages 56 and 57, reproduced on white construction for each student
- 2″ x 24″ (5 x 61 cm) construction paper
- crayons or marking pens
- scissors
- stapler

PATTERN FOR A HAPPY MASK

PATTERN FOR A SAD MASK

Pocket 5

ANCIENT ROME

CUT AND PASTE

Pocket Label, Words to Know .... **page 59**
See page 2 for information on how to prepare the pocket label. See page 10 for information on how to prepare the "Words to Know" activity.

FACT SHEET

Ancient Rome .... **page 60**
Read this background information to familiarize yourself with the ancient civilization of Rome. Share the information with your students as appropriate. Incorporate library and multimedia resources that are available.

STUDENT BOOKLET

Make an Ancient Rome Booklet .... **pages 61–63**
See page 2 for information on how to prepare the student booklet. Read and discuss the information booklet as a class. Encourage students to read their booklets to partners or independently.

ACTIVITIES

Postcard from Ancient Rome .... **page 64**
Students pretend they have visited ancient Rome and "send" a postcard to a friend. Follow the directions on page 17 for making this postcard.

Roman Puppets .... **page 65**
Students color and cut out the puppets showing typical Roman clothing. Mount the puppets on construction paper, and then attach them to craft sticks. Allow students to use the puppets to retell the story of ancient Rome.

Laurel-Wreath Crown .... **page 66**
The laurel-wreath crown was worn by a Roman emperor or by a triumphant general returning from battle as a symbol of his victory. Students make this crown to wear as a symbol of their leadership and strength.

Triumphal Arch .... **pages 67 & 68**
Ancient Romans were famous for building arches. In this activity, students make an arch of their own.

WORDS TO KNOW

See page 10 for directions.

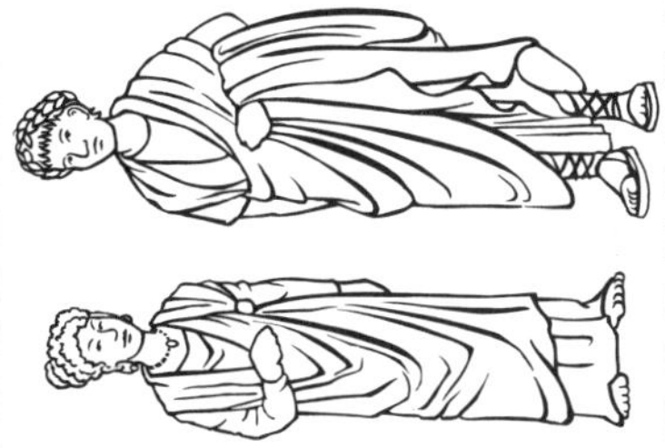

toga

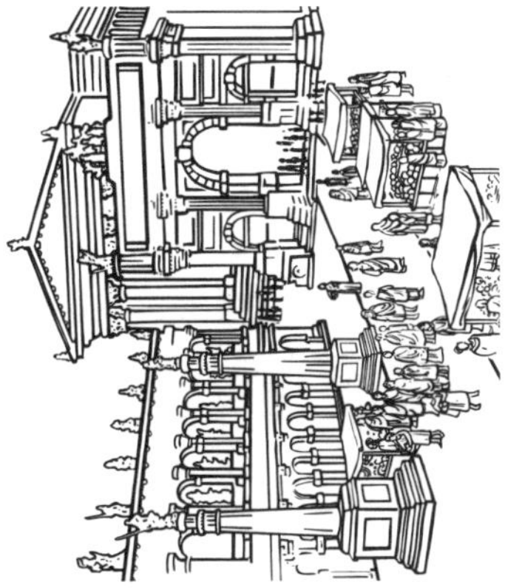

forum

I II III IV
V VI VII
VIII IX X

Roman numerals

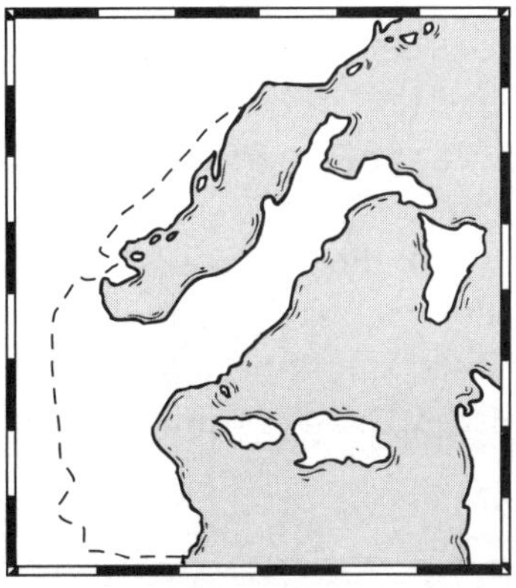

empire

FACT SHEET

ANCIENT ROME

About 753 B.C., Rome was founded as a tiny farming settlement on the banks of the Tiber River. It grew into one of the greatest empires in history. At its height, the Roman Empire spread over all the lands bordering the Mediterranean Sea. It expanded as far north as Britain and as far east as Mesopotamia. Ancient Rome was ruled by emperors. They had the help of the Senate. The Senate was a group of officials who were in charge of the army, laws, and taxes.

Rome was the biggest city in the empire. There was a square in the center of the city called the forum. There was a marketplace, government buildings, and temples in the forum. Every city had a public bath where men and women bathed separately. Theaters and amphitheaters provided plays, gladiator contests, and chariot racing for the citizens.

The Roman people belonged to different classes. Each class had different rights in the Empire. Romans were either citizens or noncitizens. Noncitizens included enslaved people, freedmen and freedwomen, women, and foreigners. Citizens included wealthy patricians (nobility), equites (businessmen), and plebeians (commoners).

FOOD

The staple food for most Romans was a type of stew made of wheat, barley, beans, or lentils. Most people bought their food from stalls in the street instead of cooking. Wealthy Romans had their own kitchens and enslaved people who cooked for them. Romans seasoned their food with a spicy fish sauce called garum. Fish parts were salted, mixed with vinegar and herbs, and left in the sun until they turned into liquid.

When wealthy Romans entertained, they ate in the triclinium, or dining room. Guests reclined on couches arranged to make three sides of a square. The guests propped themselves up on their elbows and ate with their fingers. Throughout the meal, storytellers, musicians, and jugglers entertained the guests.

SHELTER

Many Romans lived in large cities. The houses, stores, and workshops in the city were adjoined in a block of buildings. Houses were built of brick and cement. Poor people lived in rented rooms in blocks of apartments. Wealthy Romans lived in houses around courtyards and gardens. The houses looked plain from the outside. The insides of the walls were decorated with marble or painted with big murals. The floors were covered with marble or tiles. Romans had neatly laid out gardens with rows of clipped hedges and paths. Fountains, pools, and statues were also part of the gardens.

CLOTHING

Roman men, women, and children wore a simple tunic made of wool or linen with a belt around the waist. Some of the tunics had sleeves and others were sleeveless. Women's tunics reached below the knees; men's were shorter. Roman men wore togas in public. The toga was a huge semicircular, woolen sheet that was wrapped around the body and arranged in folds. Women wore many different kinds of robes and dresses over their tunics. Everyone wore leather sandals. Men wore laurel wreaths on their heads as a mark of rank. The emperor wore one as a crown.

CONTRIBUTIONS

The Romans copied many architectural styles from the Greeks. But they did invent concrete roads, the arch, vaulted domes, and aqueducts. The largest arena in the empire was the famous Colosseum where gladiators competed. The Latin language had influence on the Romance languages. The capital letters in the English alphabet are formed from the Roman alphabet. Roman numerals are used on clocks and on the cornerstones of major buildings and monuments. The names of the months also came from Rome. The names of the Roman gods and goddesses are seen in the naming of such things as the planets.

ANCIENT ROME

Ancient Rome became a big empire in A.D. 117. An **empire** is when one nation takes control of other nations. The main part of the empire was the city of Rome. In the center of the city was the forum. The **forum** had a marketplace, government buildings, and temples.

Romans started their meals with eggs and ended with fruit. They ate a type of stew made from barley, wheat, beans, and lentils. Families used olive oil, vinegar, wine, and fish sauce to season their foods. They used honey to sweeten their foods. Richer families ate fancy foods. They liked foods such as snails, dormice, stuffed olives, and peacock eggs.

The streets of ancient Rome had large apartment houses. Many of them were six stories high. They were built of brick and cement. They were dark, hot, and smoky. Rich Romans lived in large houses built of stone or brick. The houses looked plain from the outside. Inside they had big rooms filled with furniture and art. Courtyards and gardens surrounded these homes.

All Romans wore white tunics. Tunics were simple short or long gowns. They were made from wool or linen. Women wore dresses over their tunics. Rich women wore wigs, makeup, and jewelry. Some men wore togas. **Togas** were long white robes. People wore leather sandals.

The Romans were the first to use concrete to build arches and buildings. They built big arenas. They had chariot races, gladiator contests, and plays in the arenas. They built 50,000 miles (80,000 km) of paved roads. People still use **Roman numerals** for some clocks and watches.

Note: Reproduce this page for each student. Follow the directions on page 17 to make this postcard.

POSTCARD FROM ANCIENT ROME

The Colosseum was a giant outdoor arena. Gladiators put on a show for 50,000 people.

fold

Note: Reproduce this page for each student to use with the "Roman Puppets" activity, as described on page 58.

ROMAN PUPPETS

MATERIALS

- 9″ (23 cm) white paper plate
- scraps of different shades of green construction paper
- 8″ (20 cm) narrow red ribbon
- pencil
- scissors
- glue

LAUREL-WREATH CROWN

Students make this Roman symbol of military success and power. Roman men wore laurel wreaths as a mark of rank. Roman emperors wore them as crowns.

STEPS TO FOLLOW

1. Tell students which Romans were allowed to wear the laurel wreath. You may want to share with students that the Greeks also wore laurel wreaths. The winners at the Olympic Games were crowned with these kinds of wreaths.
2. Have students trim the edge off a paper plate to form the base for the crown. Then they cut a space in one side and trim the ends to make points. Younger students may need help with this step.
3. Instruct students to cut narrow leaf shapes from the green construction paper scraps as shown. (You may want to show students what laurel or bay leaves look like, and explain that we use bay leaves for cooking.)
4. Starting at one end of the wreath base, students glue the leaves onto the base. Halfway around the base, students stop and begin at the opposite end.
5. Have students tie the red ribbon around the crown at the halfway point.
6. When the glue is dry, have students write "Laurel-Wreath Crown" and their names on the back of the crown.
7. Have students wear their crowns and pretend they are emperors of Rome.

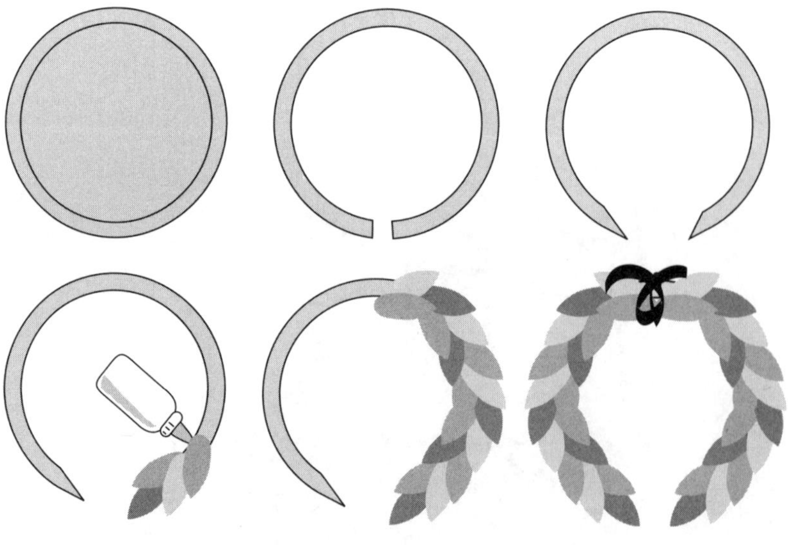

TRIUMPHAL ARCH

The arch was an important feature of Roman architecture. The arch is a curved structure that is able to support great weight. By using arches, the Romans found they could build high, strong walls using as little stone as possible.

Arches supported the waterways called aqueducts that supplied the cities with water. Arches were also built above doors, windows, and porches.

Triumphal arches were also built as tributes or monuments. When a Roman emperor or a general defeated a foreign army, the people celebrated with a parade. The Roman soldiers marched through the arch built over the street. The names of legions and their battles were carved in the stone.

Students make a model of a triumphal arch, and then draw themselves coming through it victoriously.

STEPS TO FOLLOW

1. Share the information about the use of arches in ancient Rome with students. Explain the meaning of *triumph* (victory) to students.
2. Have students read the information about Roman arches on the base of the arch pattern.
3. Instruct students to color and cut out the arch pattern.
4. Direct students to glue the arch to construction paper.
5. Tell students to write their name on the line at the top of the arch.
6. Instruct students to draw a picture of themselves in the arch opening. Explain to students that they have just had a major military victory, and all the people want to honor them.

MATERIALS

- page 68, reproduced for each student
- 9″ x 12″ (23 x 30.5 cm) construction paper
- pencil
- crayons or marking pens
- scissors
- glue

TRIUMPHAL ARCH

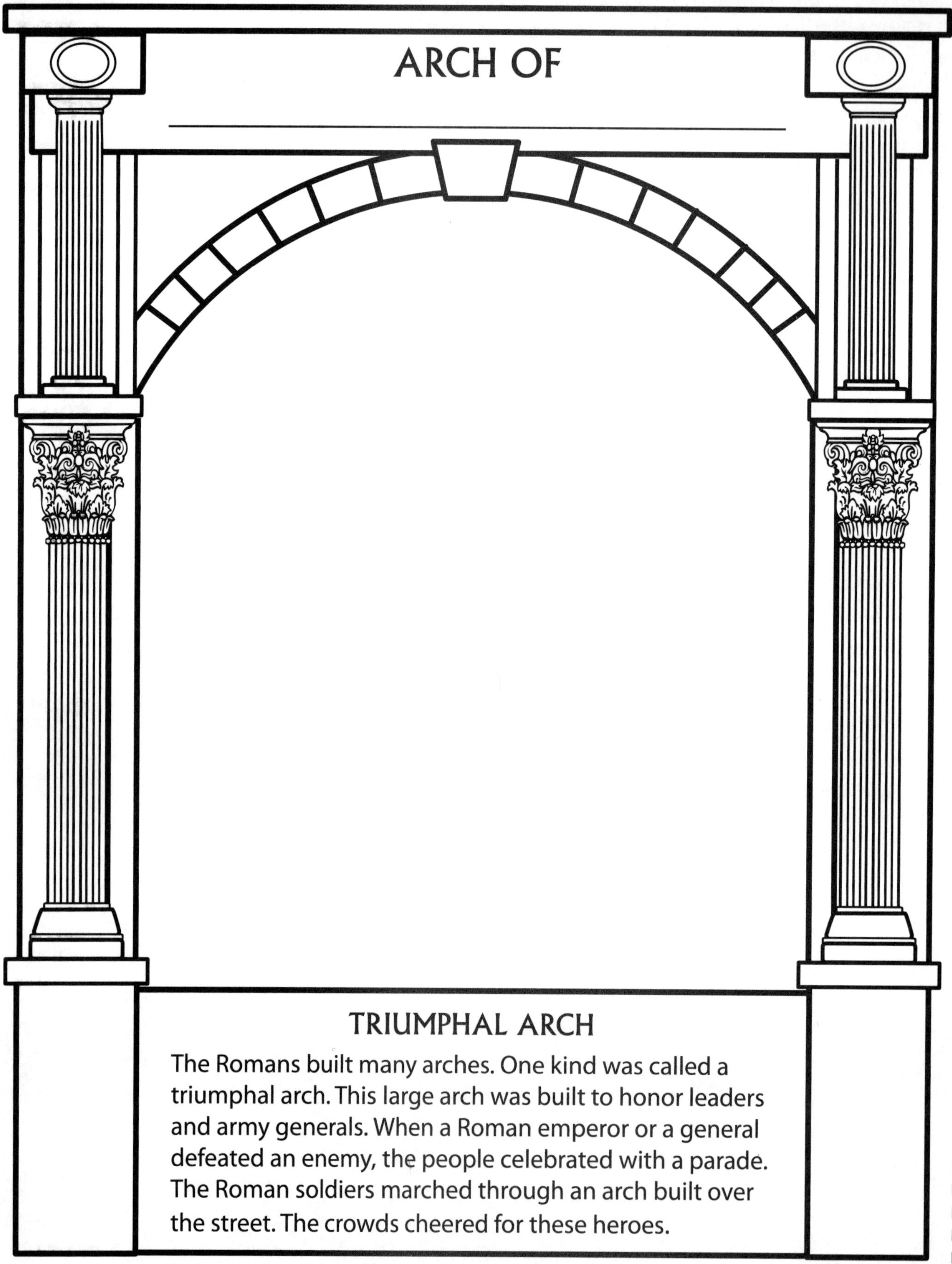

TRIUMPHAL ARCH

The Romans built many arches. One kind was called a triumphal arch. This large arch was built to honor leaders and army generals. When a Roman emperor or a general defeated an enemy, the people celebrated with a parade. The Roman soldiers marched through an arch built over the street. The crowds cheered for these heroes.

Pocket 6

ANCIENT CHINA

CUT AND PASTE

Pocket Label, Words to Know .... **page 70**
See page 2 for information on how to prepare the pocket label. See page 10 for information on how to prepare the "Words to Know" activity.

FACT SHEET

Ancient China .... **page 71**
Read this background information to familiarize yourself with the ancient civilization of China. Share the information with your students as appropriate. Incorporate library and multimedia resources that are available.

STUDENT BOOKLET

Make an Ancient China Booklet .... **pages 72–74**
See page 2 for information on how to prepare the student booklet. Read and discuss the information booklet as a class. Encourage students to read their booklets to partners or independently.

ACTIVITIES

Postcard from Ancient China .... **page 75**
Students pretend they have visited ancient China and "send" this postcard to a friend. Follow the directions on page 17 for making this postcard.

Chinese Puppets .... **page 76**
Students color and cut out the puppets showing Chinese clothing. Mount the puppets on construction paper, and then attach them to craft sticks. Allow students to use the puppets to retell the story of ancient China.

Dancing Dragon.. **pages 77 & 78**
Celebrate the Chinese New Year by making a dancing dragon. Students learn about the celebration, and then they can use the dragon to parade around the classroom.

Chinese Lanterns .... **pages 79–81**
Learn how to count to 10 in Mandarin Chinese. Students make a string of lanterns to practice counting.

WORDS TO KNOW

See page 10 for directions.

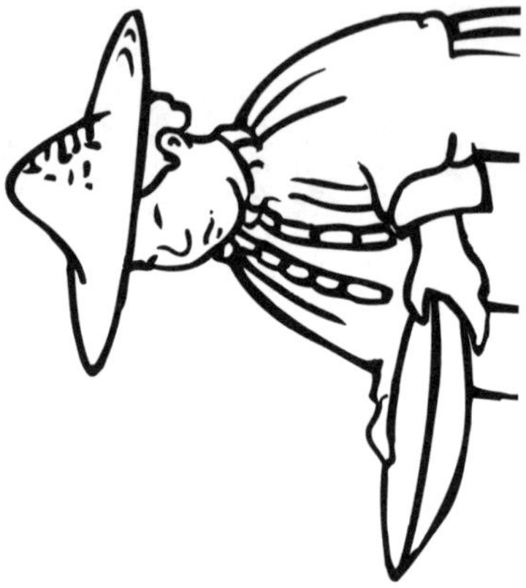

peasant

emperor

chopsticks

一 二 三
四 五 六
七 八 九

calligraphy

FACT SHEET

ANCIENT CHINA

The story of ancient China covers 11,000 years of history. That history is divided into dynasties. The Shang Dynasty is also known as the Age of Bronze. During this dynasty, artisans worked with metal in new ways. China's first emperor came to power during the Ch'in (Qin) Dynasty. Ancient China was unified during this dynasty.

During the Han Dynasty, China's boundaries were extended. All records were kept in a central place, the salt and iron mines were organized, and state factories mass-produced iron and steel tools, silk, and paper.

The T'ang Dynasty is known as the Golden Age of Ancient China. Trade moved beyond the boundaries of China. Art, music, and literature were prized.

Ancient China was surrounded by mountains, desert, and sea. The people had little contact with the rest of the world. Many of the people were farmers. They worked with wood and stone tools to grow millet and rice. The first villages grew up along the banks of the Huang He River. Soon farming spread south to the plains of the Yangtze River.

The people of ancient China were strictly divided into four main classes. The scholars and gentry could read and write. The peasants produced food on small plots. They cut terraces into the slopes of the hills. The artisans worked with their hands. The merchants were responsible for trade.

FOOD

Most people ate a simple diet of beans, grains, and vegetables. Millet, barley, wheat, and rice were steamed, boiled, or formed into noodles. Vegetables eaten included lotus roots, bamboo shoots, gourds, yams, leeks, and radishes. Meat was eaten in small quantities. Rich and poor people used spices, salt, sugar, honey, and soy sauce to flavor dishes. Food was chopped finely and cooked quickly in a wok. Food was eaten with chopsticks. Tea was a favorite drink.

SHELTER

The family was very important to ancient Chinese people. Confucius, China's greatest teacher, taught that children must be devoted to their parents. Often, many generations lived in the same house. Women lived to serve and obey their husbands. Because the Chinese believed that ancestors watched over the family, they have always made offerings to dead relatives to ensure that their souls are atpeace. Even the poorest households kept a shrine to their ancestors.

During the Han Dynasty, the rich lived in large homes and palaces made of mud and wood. In the summer, farmers lived on the land near their fields in houses made of bamboo branches. In the winter, they moved to their permanent homes in the villages. Winter homes were drafty, one-room houses with thatched or tile roofs, dirt floors, and no furniture. The walls were made of mud.

CLOTHING

Clothes identified the class of the person wearing them. High-ranking Chinese wore silk. The men wore loose robes with weighted sleeves. The women wore long skirts and jackets over short-sleeved upper garments. Peasants wore long shirt-like garments of hemp. They stuffed their clothes with paper and cloth to stay warm in the winter. Shoes were very important during T'ang times. Peasants wore straw sandals. Nobles wore fine cloth slippers.

CONTRIBUTIONS

Ancient China is known for its many inventions. They invented such everyday things as paper, kites, yo-yos, jump ropes, and umbrellas. They were the first to invent gunpowder, the compass, the wheelbarrow, and the earthquake detector. Early Chinese people discovered how to combine certain herbs for medicine. They made the first real porcelain pottery. For centuries, only the Chinese knew how to make silk.

ANCIENT CHINA

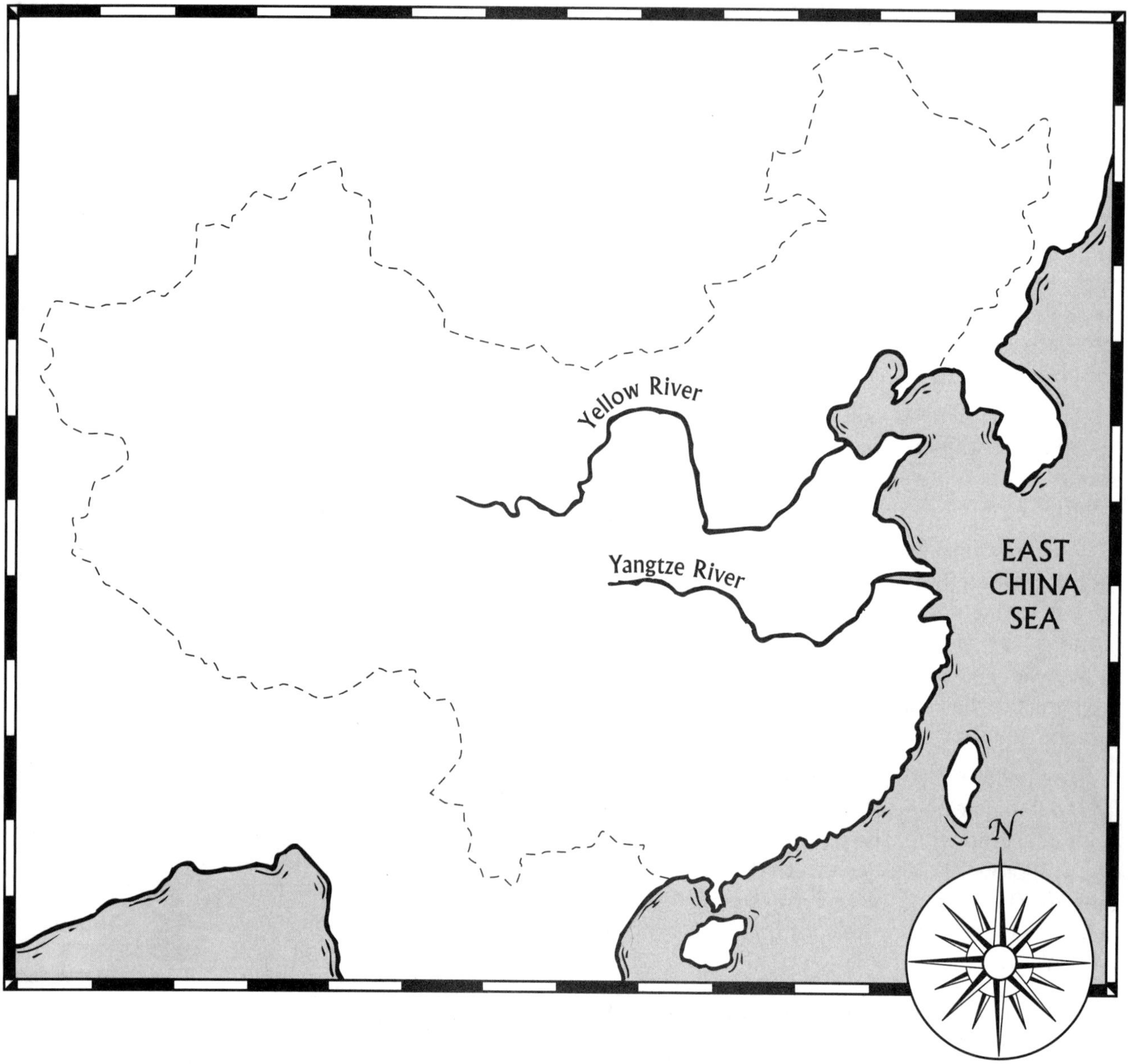

Ancient China began around the Huang He River (also called the Yellow River). It grew into a large civilization. Ancient China was surrounded by the Himalaya Mountains and the Gobi Desert. The Chinese built the Great Wall of China to keep invaders out. These things made travel to other parts of the world difficult. The people of ancient China had to invent many things for themselves.

In the southern part of China, people ate rice, steamed dumplings, and fish. In the north they ate wheat noodles instead of rice. They liked vegetables such as bamboo shoots, leeks, and radishes. They also ate fruits such as plums, oranges, and peaches. They used salt, soy sauce, sugar, ginger, and garlic to season foods. **Chopsticks** were used to pick up the food to eat. Their favorite drink was hot tea.

Farmers lived in one- or two-story mud houses. They had tile or thatched roofs. People in the city lived in cramped mud houses close to each other. The rich lived in large homes that were built around courtyards. The **emperors** lived in palaces. The Chinese believed it was good to have grandparents, parents, and children all living together.

Rich people wore colorful silk shirts and pants. They also wore fancy silk robes with long sleeves. The rich wore fine cloth slippers. Only the emperor could wear the color yellow. **Peasant** farmers wore long shirtlike garments over short pants. Their clothes were made of rough plant fibers. Peasants wore straw sandals.

The Chinese were the first to learn how to make silk. They invented paper. They wrote in beautiful **calligraphy**. They made gunpowder and fireworks. They invented the compass and the wheelbarrow. They made the first earthquake detector. They also made fun toys such as kites, yo-yos, and jump ropes.

一 二 三

四 五 六

七 八 九

Note: Reproduce this page for each student. Follow the directions on page 17 to make this postcard.

POSTCARD FROM ANCIENT CHINA

The Great Wall of China was built to keep invaders out. Most of the Great Wall of China still stands today. The total length of the Great Wall was over 13,000 miles (20,921 km).

fold

Note: Reproduce this page for each student to use with the "Chinese Puppets" activity, as described on page 69.

CHINESE PUPPETS

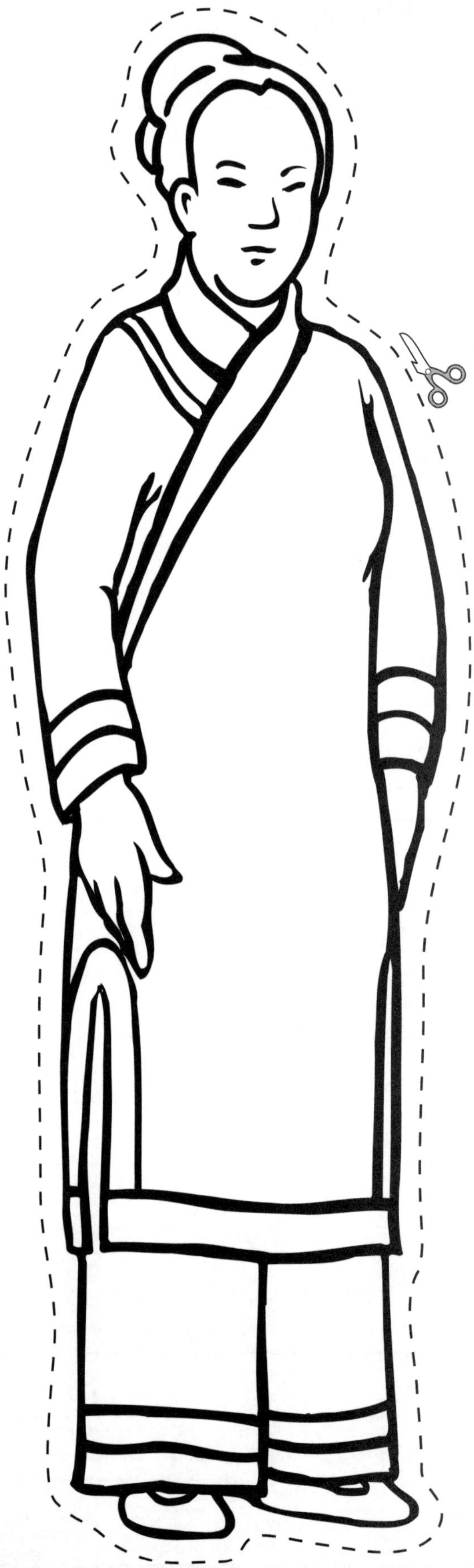

DANCING DRAGON

The Chinese New Year begins on the first day of the first lunar month. The dates for the Chinese New Year vary from January 21 to February 19. The celebration is also called the Spring Festival. The Spring Festival began in ancient times as a time when China's farmers gave thanks for the rich land right before the spring planting season.

Today the Chinese New Year is a time to pay off debts, settle disputes, and make a new start. During the festival, family and friends exchange gifts of cakes, candy, and oranges. Children receive money in little red packets. Families clean their homes and hang good luck banners in front of their homes. They also have a parade led by dragon and lion dancers.

Students make a Chinese New Year dragon to learn about the celebration.

STEPS TO FOLLOW

1. Share the information about the Chinese New Year with students. Explain that they are going to make a dancing dragon for a Chinese New Year parade.
2. Direct students to accordion-fold the construction paper as shown.
3. Have students color and cut out the dragon head and facts.
4. Students then glue the dragon head to the first panel and the facts to the other panels, placing the invitation to celebrate last.
5. Have students cut out a red tail for the dragon and glue it to the edge of the last panel.
6. Glue craft sticks to both ends of the dragon. Allow to dry.
7. Now the dragon is ready to lead the parade.

Steps 2, 5, & 6

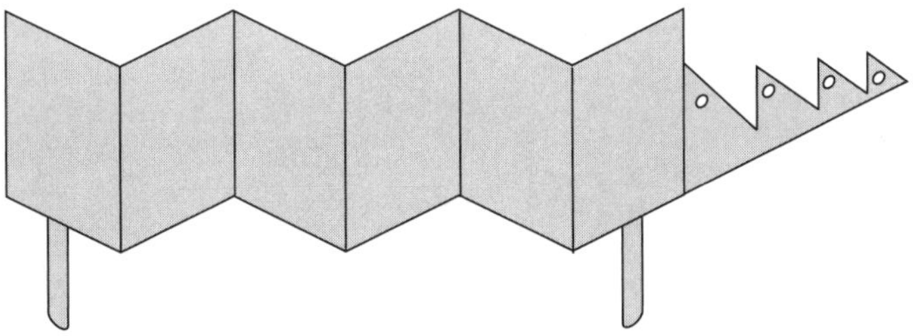

MATERIALS

- page 78, reproduced for each student
- 4″ x 18″ (10 x 45.5 cm) red construction paper
- scraps of red construction paper
- two crafts sticks
- crayons
- scissors
- glue

DANCING DRAGON

CELEBRATE
THE
NEW YEAR!

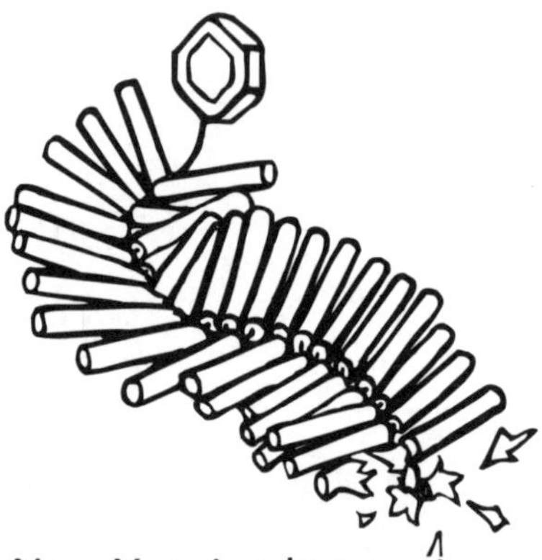

The New Year is a happy time. It is time to make a fresh start. Firecrackers are set off.

People put on new clothes. They clean their houses. They hang good luck banners.

They visit family and friends. They give cakes, candy, and oranges. Children get money in red packets.

They have a big parade. Dragon dancers lead the parade. The dragon brings good luck.

CHINESE LANTERNS

The New Year celebrations last for 15 days. At the end of the 15 days, the Chinese celebrate with the Lantern Festival. Lanterns are hung to welcome in spring. Thousands of brightly colored paper lanterns are hung along the streets of China. In ancient China, this festival was held to celebrate the end of a cold winter and the beginning of a warm spring.

Students make paper lanterns to help them learn how to count in Chinese.

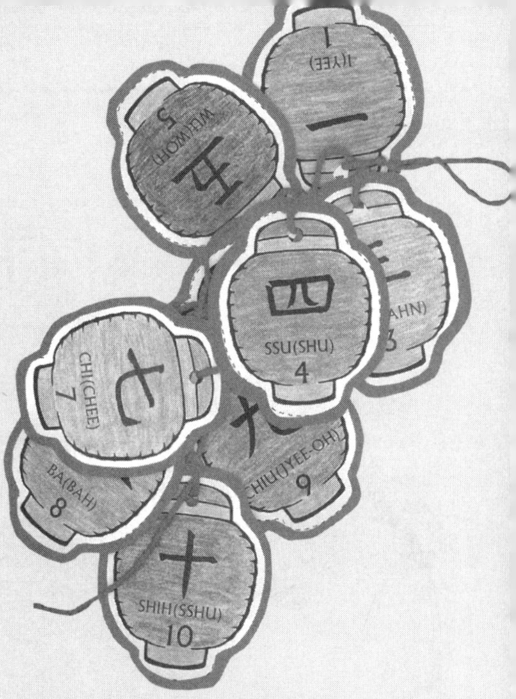

STEPS TO FOLLOW

1. Discuss the Lantern Festival with students. Then talk about how they are going to learn how to count to 10 in Chinese (Mandarin).
2. Have students cut apart the Chinese calligraphy numbers and glue them to construction paper. Allow to dry.
3. Direct students to cut around the shapes, and then punch a hole in each shape.
4. Before hanging the lanterns, instruct students to practice saying the 10 numbers with a partner.
5. Then have students tie the lanterns to the red yarn. Thread the lanterns one at a time. Make a loose knot each time to hold the lanterns in place. The string of lanterns may be displayed in the classroom.
6. When finished displaying the lanterns, have students gently fold the string of lanterns together to place in the pocket.
7. Optional: Extend the lesson by having students copy the Chinese numbers in black crayon on writing paper.

MATERIALS

- pages 80 and 81, reproduced for each student
- two 9" x 12" (23 x 30.5 cm) sheets of red construction paper
- 36" (91.5 cm) red yarn
- crayons
- scissors
- glue
- hole punch
- Optional: black crayon and writing paper

CHINESE LANTERN PATTERNS

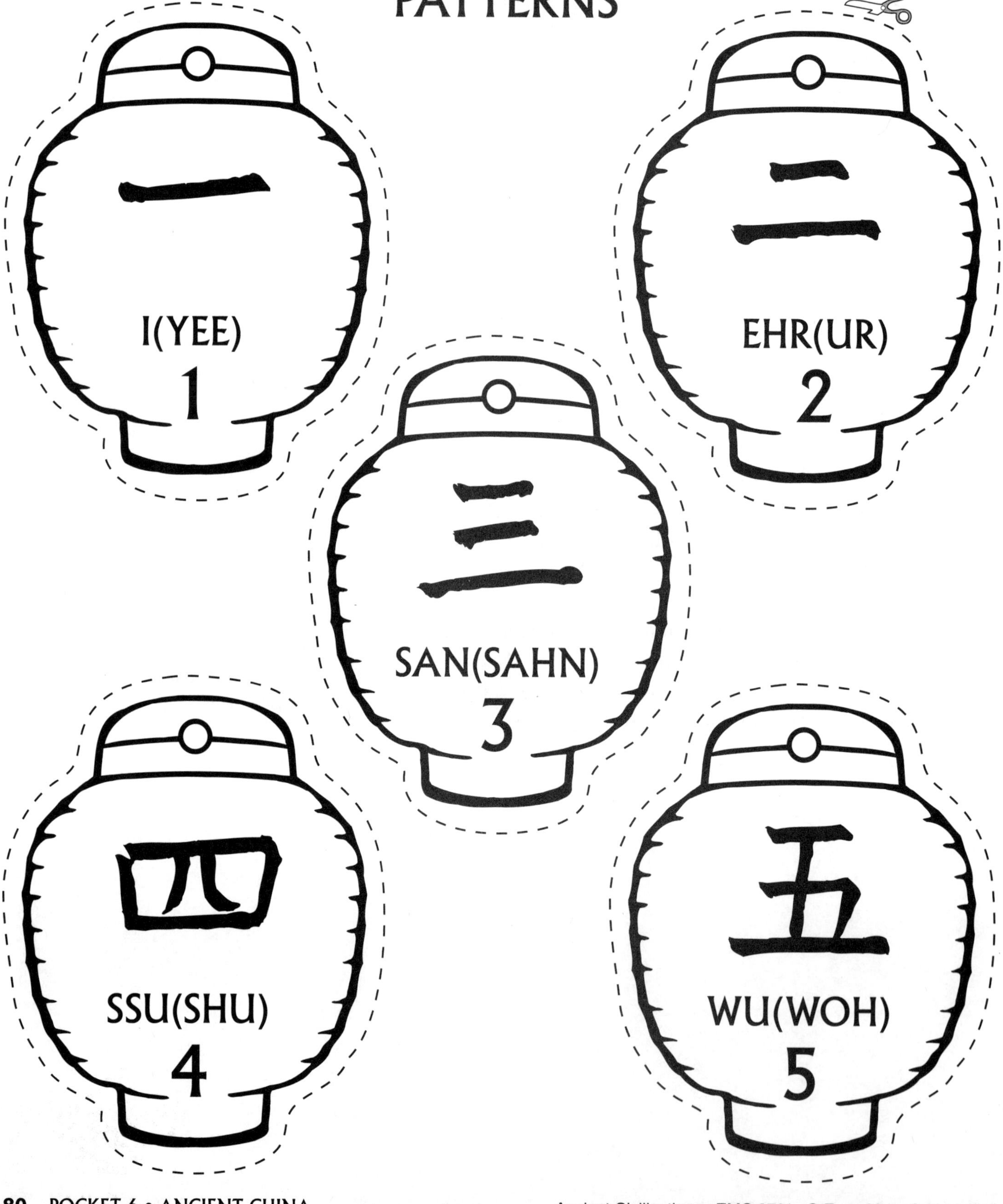

CHINESE LANTERN PATTERNS

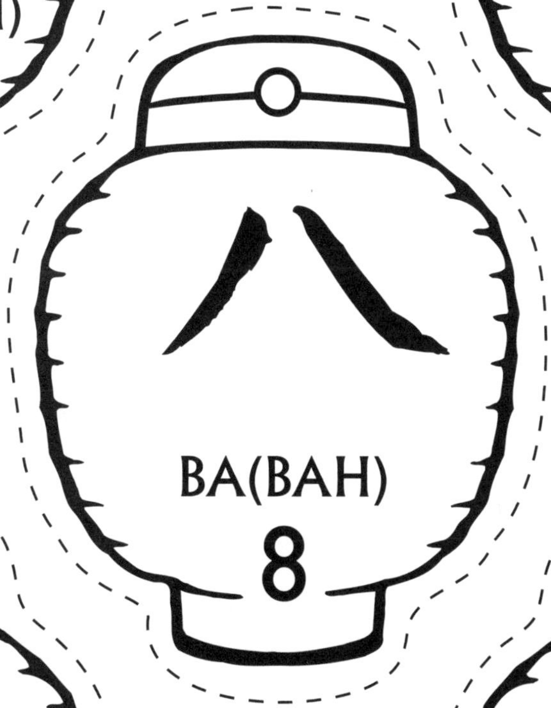

Pocket 7

ANCIENT AZTEC WORLD

CUT AND PASTE

Pocket Label, Words to Know............... **page 83**
See page 2 for information on how to prepare the pocket label. See page 10 for information on how to prepare the "Words to Know" activity.

FACT SHEET

Ancient Aztec World........................ **page 84**
Read this background information to familiarize yourself with the ancient civilization of the Aztecs. Share the information with your students as appropriate. Incorporate library and multimedia resources that are available.

STUDENT BOOKLET

Ancient Aztec World Booklet.......... **pages 85–87**
See page 2 for information on how to prepare the student booklet. Read and discuss the information booklet as a class. Encourage students to read their booklets to partners or independently.

ACTIVITIES

Postcard from the Ancient Aztec World.... **page 88**
Students pretend they have visited the ancient Aztecs and "send" this postcard to a friend. Follow the directions on page 17 for making this postcard.

Aztec Puppets............................. **page 89**
Students color and cut out the puppets showing Aztec clothing. Mount the puppets on construction paper, and then attach them to craft sticks. Allow students to use the puppets to retell the story of the Aztecs.

Aztec Calendar... **pages 90–92**
Create a 20-day sun calendar using unusual Aztec symbols for each day of the month. Students then decide which symbol they would have liked to be born under.

A Feather Fan... **page 93**
The Aztecs used exotic bird feathers to decorate their clothing and to make fans. Students make their own feather fan to cool themselves in the classroom.

ANCIENT AZTEC WORLD

WORDS TO KNOW

See page 10 for directions.

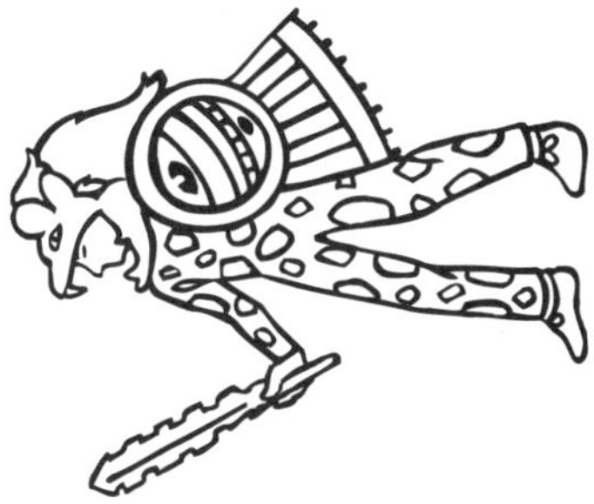

knight

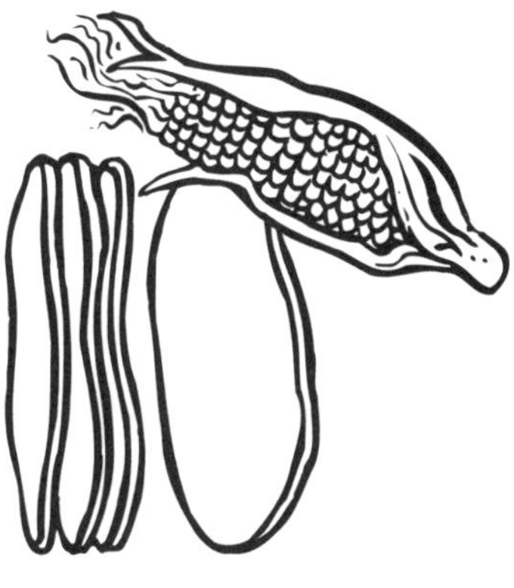

tortillas

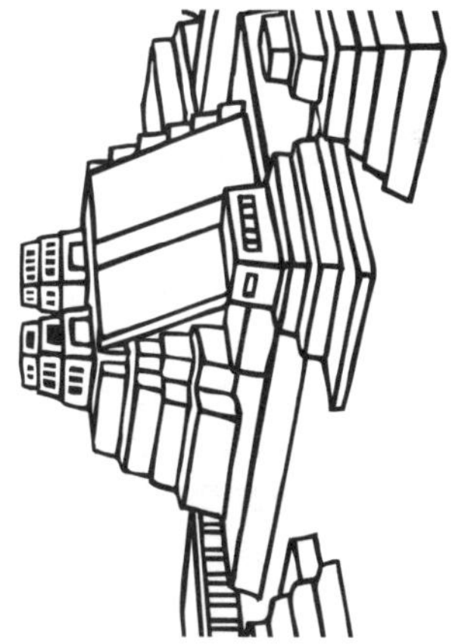

temple

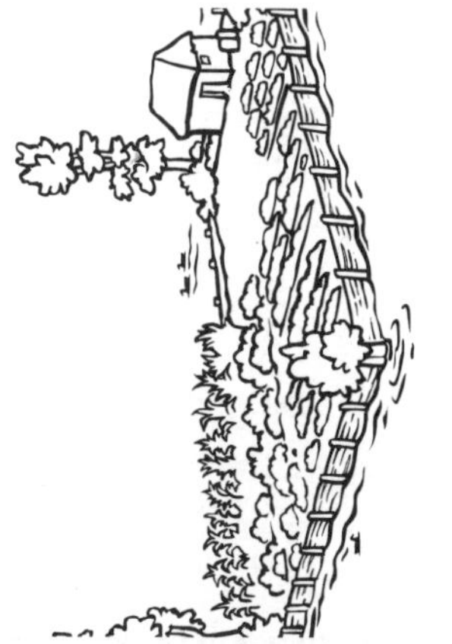

chinampas

FACT SHEET

ANCIENT AZTEC WORLD

The Aztec period stretches from A.D. 1300 to 1500. The Aztecs' homeland was the great central valley of modern Mexico. It is a land of contrasts. There are snowy peaks, tropical rainforests, sandy beaches, smoking volcanoes, and windswept steppes. According to legend, the early Aztecs were told by their god Huitzilopochtli to look for a sign—an eagle grasping a snake perched on a prickly-pear cactus. If they settled where they saw this sign, they would become rich and powerful. The Aztecs found the spot described by the god on a swampy island in Lake Texcoco. They built a village of reed huts and called their settlement Tenochtitlán.

The Aztecs worked hard. They reclaimed land from the lake by building floating gardens called chinampas. The village prospered. The Aztecs became rich and powerful. They conquered other people in the region and took over their land. This was the beginning of the Aztec empire.

By A.D. 1500, Tenochtitlán was probably the largest city in the world. About half a million people lived there. The city was crisscrossed by a network of canals and linked to the mainland by three stone causeways. The great central square was the hub of the empire.

Most people in the empire were farmers. The farmer's main tool was a long stick flattened at one end. It was used to turn the soil, plant seeds, and pull out weeds. Huge amounts of food had to be produced to feed all the people of the empire. The main crops were corn, beans, squash, amaranth, and chili peppers.

FOOD

Aztec legends say that the Aztecs lived on snakes and cactus at first. Farmers soon grew most of their food supply on their floating islands. Corn was the most important crop.

People ate nothing when they got up. They had breakfast around ten o'clock after several hours of work. Breakfast was usually a bowl of corn porridge flavored with honey or pepper. The main meal was at midday. Meat was eaten only for special occasions. People ate lots of vegetables such as beans, tomatoes, and sweet potatoes. There were always freshly made tortillas. Everything was washed down with water.

SHELTER

Farmers lived in mud-brick huts that had thatched roofs. People in the cities lived in low, flat-roofed houses built of mud-bricks. The poor had only one room. Their simple homes were built around a central courtyard and bordered by a canal on one side. The walls were whitewashed and the floors were hard earth. Houses were built in neat rows along carefully planned streets.

The rich lived in vast stone palaces with dozens of different rooms, airy courtyards, and beautiful gardens. Everyone (the rich and the poor) sat and slept on woven reed mats on the floor.

CLOTHING

There were strict rules about Aztec clothes and jewelry that separated the rich from the poor, nobles from common people. Only nobles could wear clothes made from feathers and soft, silky cotton and jewels. Common people wore clothes woven from the rough fibers of the maguey cactus.

Aztec women and girls wore loose blouses and skirts. Men and boys wore loincloths and cloaks knotted on one shoulder.

CONTRIBUTIONS

The Aztecs are remembered for their chinampas (floating gardens) where they produced huge amounts of food. Corn was the main crop, along with beans and squash. The Aztecs are noted for introducing foods such as chili peppers, tortillas, and chocolate to the world. Words such as *coyote*, *guacamole*, and *gum* come from the main Aztec language called *Nahuatl*.

ANCIENT AZTEC WORLD

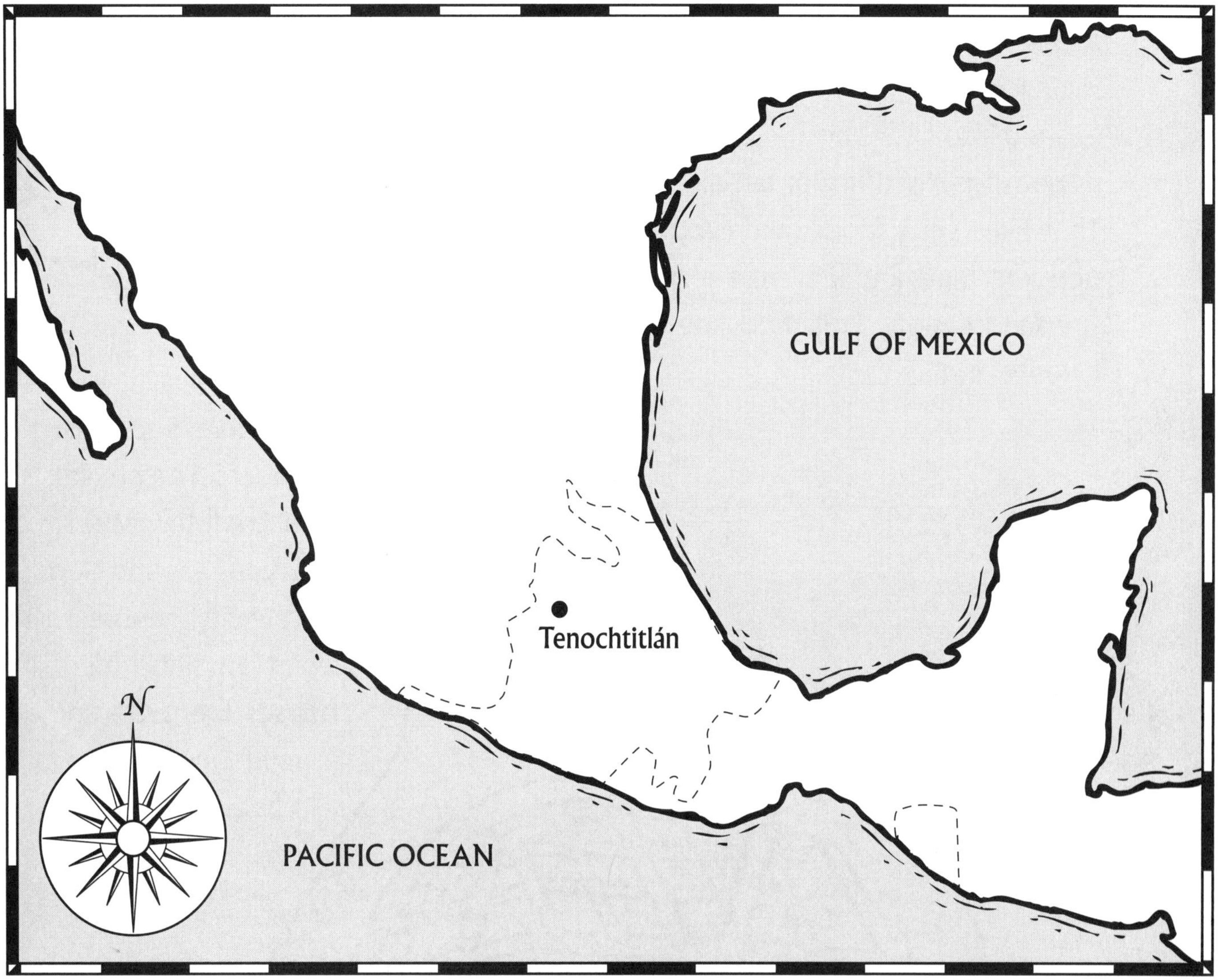

The Aztecs lived in an area we now call Mexico. They built a mighty empire about 800 years ago. The Aztec Empire had hundreds of towns and cities. More than 5 million people lived in the area. The capital city was called Tenochtitlán (teh-notch-teet-lahn). The capital was on an island in the middle of Lake Texcoco.

The Aztec people ate two meals a day. Corn was the main food. The corn was ground into flour and cooked as porridge, **tortillas**, or tamales. They liked spicy foods made with hot chili peppers. Meat and fish were served only on special occasions. Hot chocolate was their favorite drink.

Most farmers lived in simple mud-brick huts. They had thatched roofs. The houses were plain inside. They had whitewashed walls and dirt floors. Everyone sat and slept on woven reed mats. In the city, people lived in low, flat-roofed houses. Emperors and richer people lived in palaces.

An Aztec man wore a loincloth and a cloak. An Aztec woman wore a long, loose skirt and a baggy tunic on top. The clothes were made from cactus plants. Richer people wore clothes made from feathers and cotton. Warriors wore tunics. They had to prove their bravery in battle. Then they were called **knights** and got to wear jaguar or eagle costumes.

The Aztecs built floating gardens called **chinampas**. Chinampas were built right in the middle of a lake. They grew vegetables, fruits, and flowers there. Thanks to the Aztecs, we enjoy foods such as tortillas, chili peppers, and chocolate. The Aztecs built beautiful **temples** to honor the gods.

Note: Reproduce this page for each student. Follow the directions on page 17 to make this postcard.

POSTCARD FROM ANCIENT AZTEC WORLD

The Great Temple in Tenochtitlán was built to honor the Aztec gods.

fold

Note: Reproduce this page for each student to use with the "Aztec Puppets" activity, as described on page 82.

AZTEC PUPPETS

AN AZTEC CALENDAR

The Aztecs created different calendars. The Aztecs used one calendar based on 260 days. Historians believe that this calendar was based on how many days a baby takes to develop before it is born. There were 13 months with 20 days in each month. They had symbols to represent each day of the month. Babies were often named after the symbol for the day of the month on which they were born. Farmers used a calendar based on the movements of the sun. That calendar had 360 days. A third kind of calendar had 584 days, which included special festival days.

Students create their own 20-day calendar using Aztec symbols for each day. Then students decide which symbol they would have liked to be born under.

MATERIALS

- pages 91 and 92, reproduced for each student
- 10" (25.5 cm) tagboard circle
- crayons
- scissors
- glue

STEPS TO FOLLOW

1. Talk about how the Aztec calendar was used and compare it to the one we use today.
2. Have students color and cut out the sun pattern.
3. Direct students to glue the sun to the tagboard circle, leaving about a 2" (5 cm) border.
4. Instruct students to color and cut out the animal symbol strips.
5. Have students arrange the animal symbols around the sun and glue them into place.
6. On the back of the calendar, have students write which symbol they would have liked to be born under and why.

AZTEC CALENDAR

AZTEC CALENDAR

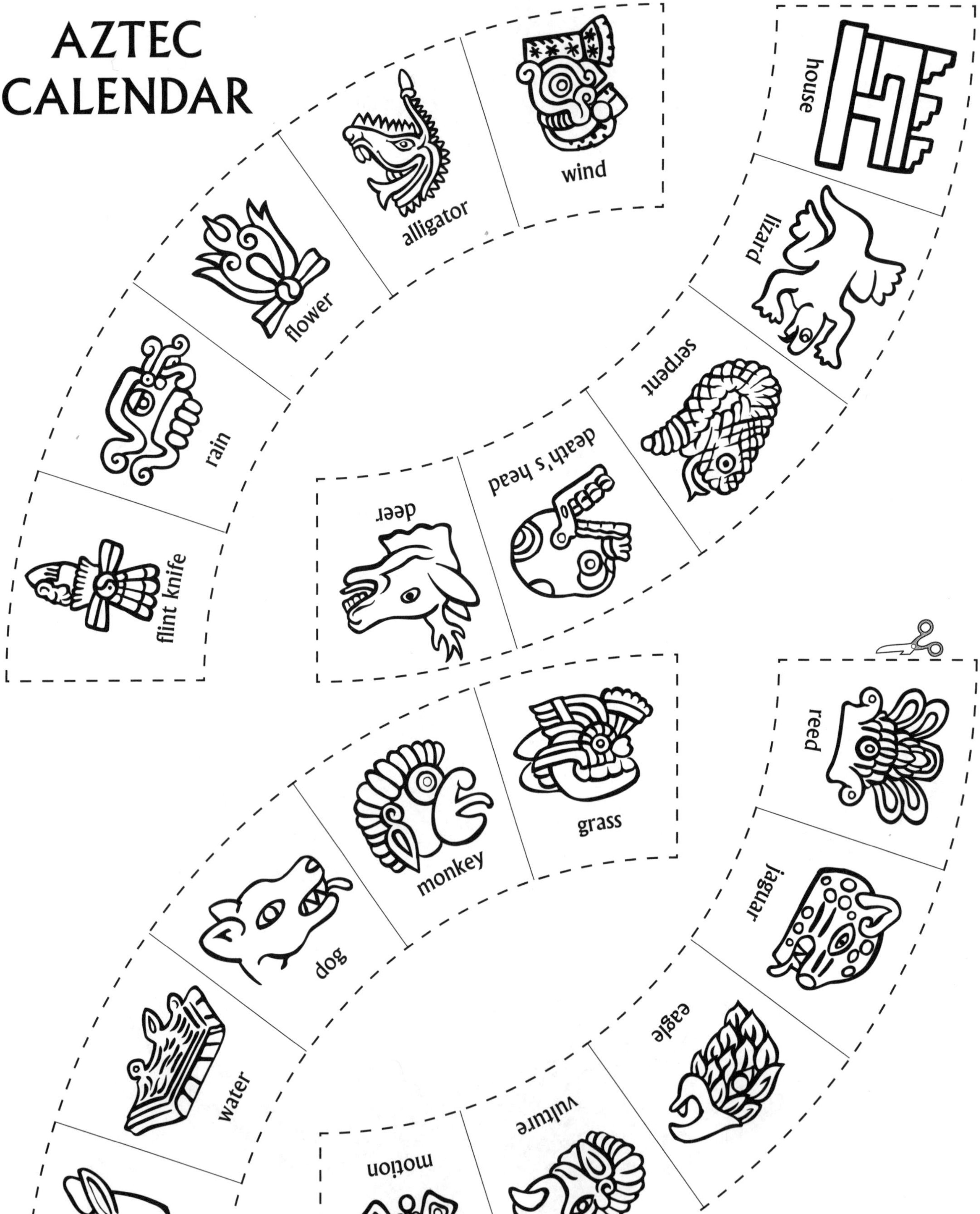

A FEATHER FAN

Aztec nobles and triumphant warriors decorated their clothes with colorful feathers and used feather fans to cool themselves. This model may be made from construction paper feathers, real feathers, or a combination of the two. This mini-fan is much smaller than the ones used by the Aztecs.

STEPS TO FOLLOW

1. Have students slip the large circle between the craft sticks and glue them together. This forms the base and handle of the fan.
2. Direct students to cut 5″ (13 cm) paper feathers from the scraps as shown. Students may notch the edges if desired.

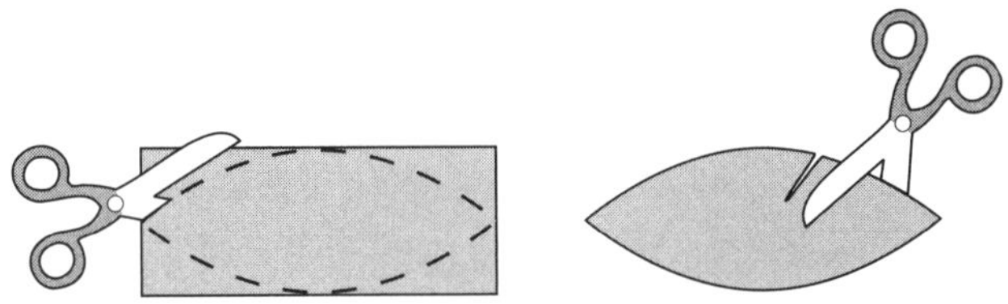

3. Students then glue the feathers onto the larger circle until it is completely covered. You may choose to allow students to add a few real feathers to the fan.
4. Have students glue the smaller circle in the center of the fan to hold the feathers in place.
5. Allow students to fan each other as they discuss the Aztecs.

MATERIALS

- 6″ (15 cm) circle cut from posterboard or a paper plate
- 2″ x 5″ (5 x 13 cm) construction paper scraps
- 2″ (5 cm) construction paper circle
- two craft sticks
- glue
- scissors
- Optional: real feathers

MATERIALS

- pages 95 and 96, reproduced for each student
- 4" x 5" (10 x 13 cm) construction paper
- pencil
- crayons
- scissors
- glue
- stapler

EVALUATION

Now that students have completed all seven pockets, use this evaluation project to help them review and remember the ancient civilizations. Students make a passport of all the places they have visited in this book.

STEPS TO FOLLOW

1. Tell students that when people travel to other places in the world, they carry a passport with them. Review the six civilizations and ask students to think of one thing they liked about each culture.
2. Have students fill out the passport information first.
3. Then direct students to draw and write about a favorite part of each civilization, using the patterns provided.
4. Instruct students to cut apart the cover, passport information, and six civilization cards.
5. Direct students to glue the cover onto the construction paper.
6. Have students stack the pages in order and staple them together to make a passport booklet.
7. Encourage students to share their passports with the class.
8. Store passports in the first pocket.

STUDENT PASSPORT PATTERNS

My PASSPORT to the ANCIENT CIVILIZATIONS

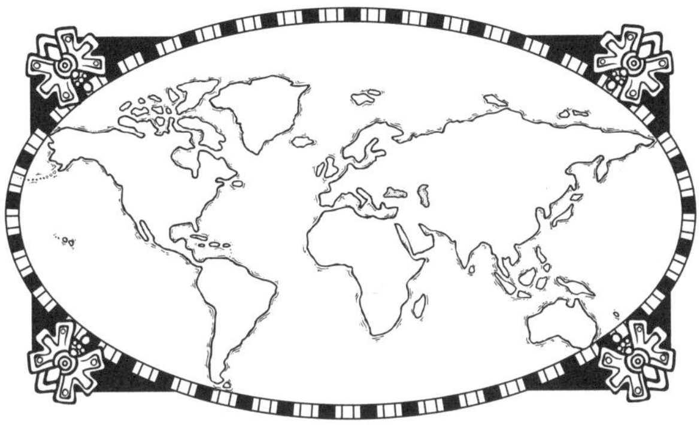

Name ____________________

This passport belongs to:

Name: ____________________

Address: ____________________

____

Date of Birth: ____________________

picture or photo of student

2

Ancient Mesopotamia

I liked ____________________

____

3

Ancient Egypt

I liked ____________________

____

4

STUDENT PASSPORT PATTERNS

Ancient Greece

I liked ______________________________

____

5

Ancient Rome

I liked ______________________________

____

6

Ancient China

I liked ______________________________

____

7

Ancient Aztec World

I liked ______________________________

____

8